SERVE REFLECT REPEAT

Compiled by: Rachel Ogorek
Forward by: Leslie Lenkowsky
Edited by: Kate Camara
Cover Illustration by: Eric N. Walton

authorHOUSE®

AuthorHouse™
1663 Liberty Drive
Bloomington, IN 47403
www.authorhouse.com
Phone: 1-800-839-8640

Published by AuthorHouse 09/09/2014

ISBN: 978-1-4969-3487-1 (sc)
ISBN: 978-1-4969-3486-4 (e)

For everyone who has worn the "A"

Contents

The Many Faces of AmeriCorps

In his book on the passage of the National and Community Service Act of 1993, Steven Waldman refers to AmeriCorps as "the public policy equivalent of a Swiss army knife, performing numerous useful functions in one affordable package."[1] The many kinds of activities AmeriCorps members undertake – and the many kinds of benefits they seek to provide – have been important strengths of the program. As the stories in this volume suggest, in the past two decades, AmeriCorps members have served communities in almost every

> " What exactly is AmeriCorps and why is it worth having? "

imaginable way and helped people of all ages and backgrounds. They have also helped themselves, not only by earning money for further education, but also by acquiring skills and outlooks that have shaped their lives.

These stories are inspiring and by no means, untypical. I heard many like them when I served first, as a board of directors member, and then, as CEO of the Corporation for National and Community Service, or CNCS, the Federal agency that sponsors AmeriCorps. I also saw AmeriCorps members at work throughout the United States, giving generously of their time and effort.

But stories can only go so far. The many faces of AmeriCorps also pose a challenge for the program. Its identity is not always clear and its accomplishments, harder to see. Twenty years after its creation, AmeriCorps enjoys a favorable reputation in the minds of Americans;

but because its public support is wide, but not deep, it has grown slowly and still faces efforts to abolish it entirely.

What exactly is AmeriCorps and why is it worth having?

The Roots of AmeriCorps[2]

AmeriCorps was not created until 1993, however its roots stretch back over a century. Although the rationale has changed with the times, the goal has remained consistent: engaging more Americans in addressing pressing national (and international) problems.

Edward Bellamy's late 19th-century utopian novel, *Looking Backward*, envisioned an army of civilian workers providing public services. A few years later, in an influential 1906 essay, the Harvard philosopher, psychologist, and pacifist, William James, called national service "the moral equivalent of war." In the event nations agreed to stop fighting one another, he suggested, it could provide an acceptable alternative to combat for the young men who might otherwise have become soldiers.

During the Depression, Franklin Delano Roosevelt, created the Civilian Conservation Corps (CCC), generally regarded as the first non-military national service program in the United States. Responding to the problems created by high unemployment, especially among young, urban men, it recruited an estimated three million participants between 1933 and 1942, when it was phased out because of American involvement in the Second World War. Based in rural camps and under military-like discipline, the Corps members completed a wide range of conservation, public works, and historical preservation projects, receiving $30 monthly, plus food, clothing and medical care for their efforts.

The next national service program was really an *international* one. During his presidential campaign, John F. Kennedy asked college students to "contribute" their lives to serving their country as a way of demonstrating that a "free society can compete" with its adversaries. This eventually led to the creation of the Peace Corps, which now enlists Americans (of all ages) for two-year assignments in developing countries throughout the world, pays participants a living allowance and medical benefits, and gives them a cash award upon completion of their service. Over 200,000 people have participated since the program was created in 1961, though annually, less than 7500 Peace Corps members serve, far below original expectations.

As part of the "war on poverty," President Lyndon B. Johnson returned the idea of national service to domestic policy. In 1965, he created Volunteers in Service to America (VISTA). (The Johnson administration also created two programs for senior citizens, Foster Grandparents and Senior Companions, which give small stipends to their members.) Participants were assigned to help organizations in low-income communities and received modest stipends and fringe benefits, as well as end-of-service awards. VISTA too has remained small – about 7500 members now serve each year – and in 1993, became a component of AmeriCorps.

During the Vietnam War, as opposition to the military draft grew, proposals for more ambitious national service programs were made, partly to offer an alternative for draft-eligible students to serving in the armed forces. With the abolition of the military draft and the advent of a smaller, "all-volunteer" force, concerns that young people might not be asked to shoulder the burdens of citizenship prompted calls for civilian service initiatives, including from prominent scholars and intellectuals, such as Charles C. Moskos and William F. Buckley, Jr.

The AmeriCorps program we know today stemmed from yet another rationale. Seeking to project a "kinder, gentler" image than his predecessor, President George H.W. Bush pledged to seek ways to help charities – "a thousand points of light," as he called them – play a more active role in dealing with the nation's social, health, environmental and other problems. In 1990, that led to the creation of a "Commission on National and Community Service," which made a series of demonstration grants to examine the potential of national service as a tool for addressing these needs.

Campaigning against Bush in 1992, however, William J. Clinton criticized the incumbent for paying insufficient attention to the difficulties facing lower- and middle-class Americans. Among them, in his view, was the rising cost of higher education. To help hard-pressed college and university students, he called for a program that would enable them to work off the expenses of their schooling by making a commitment to serve their country for a year or two.

After taking office, Clinton recognized that the costs of a program which could annually enroll the millions of young people graduating from colleges and universities each year would be enormous. College and university presidents also resisted the idea, favoring a simple increase in federal scholarships and loans for higher education instead. Consequently, the White House scaled back its proposal and AmeriCorps was born.

AmeriCorps Today

AmeriCorps is essentially a program of grants to non-profit organizations that enable them to recruit and compensate people who serve on their staffs. Most of the awards are made by the federal government (through CNCS), but part of the program's funds are allocated by state "service commissions," appointed by governors. The Clinton administration initially obtained funding for 25,000 positions for AmeriCorps members, but increased the total to 50,000 before leaving office. In 2004, President George W. Bush expanded the program again to 75,000 participants. The Edward M. Kennedy Serve America Act, passed in 2009, called for further growth to 250,000 members, but Congress has not appropriated funds for more than 100,000. Half of these are positions in which AmeriCorps members serve less than full-time.

In addition, there are two smaller components of AmeriCorps. VISTA is operated directly by CNCS, through federal offices in each state. The National Civilian Community Corps (NCCC), which has 1200 participants, is also run by

> From one perspective, AmeriCorps' broad range of activities and members can be seen as an advantage, since participants can be deployed to best meet the needs of local communities and organizations and to utilize effectively their particular skills.

CNCS through five camps, located throughout the United States. In his 2015 budget proposal, President Obama requested funds to integrate Foster Grandparents and Senior Companions with AmeriCorps.

Perhaps the most important consequence of this structure is that there is not a single AmeriCorps program or AmeriCorps experience in the United States, but thousands. Except for the two Federally-run components, organizations that want to recruit members have to apply, following guidelines issued by CNCS and the state commissions, which typically specify broad areas of policy interest (such as improving reading skills among low-income children or helping homeless veterans). AmeriCorps is, in effect, a program of support for American charities, limited to allowing them to obtain short-term employees for their staffs. Since expenditures for staff are usually the largest budget item for non-profit groups, this kind of assistance can be very valuable. Indeed, some large organizations such as City Year, Teach for America, JumpStart, Public Allies and Habitat for Humanity, annually win multiple awards from CNCS or its state affiliates and may enroll thousands of AmeriCorps members.

Another result is that AmeriCorps members perform a wide variety of tasks. Although all participants can receive monthly stipends to help defray living costs, health insurance, and upon completion of their period of service, an award that can be used to repay student loans or for further education, what they actually do varies considerably, depending on the AmeriCorps grantee with which they are serving.

Some programs focus on directly providing services, such as tutoring or staffing health clinics, while others involve AmeriCorps members in managing community volunteers and building the capacity of nonprofit organizations. Some grantees target specific communities or populations, including faith-based ones, while others deploy AmeriCorps participants to multiple locations or populations for brief periods of intensive activity. Some are run in a quasi-military manner, while others operate informally. Some have in-service training programs for members, while others do little to develop the skills of participants. In recent years, some have specialized in responding to natural disasters, such as floods and hurricanes, while others have assisted with government programs, such as the Department of Education's School Turnaround initiative.

AmeriCorps members also come from a wide variety of backgrounds. Since some programs focus on creating service opportunities for disadvantaged groups, they try to recruit people who might be able to use a structured service experience to get back on track in their schooling or the labor market. Others, such as the best-known AmeriCorps program, Teach for America, target high-achieving college graduates who see an extended service experience as an important milestone in career or personal development.

> "Since it was created twenty years ago, AmeriCorps has aimed to provide valuable services to communities, while also having a lifelong impact on the lives of its participants."

From one perspective, AmeriCorps' broad range of activities and members can be seen as an advantage, since participants can be deployed to best meet the needs of local communities and organizations and to utilize effectively their particular skills. That is why a "Swiss army knife" became an often-used metaphor.

But AmeriCorps programs rarely look alike and members rarely have common experiences, or even much sense that they are part of the same program. Since each has its own identity to maintain, AmeriCorps grantees may not always advertise their participation in the program either. Indeed, some are better-known and more admired than AmeriCorps itself.

As a result, despite the kinds of testimonials in this volume, judging what AmeriCorps is accomplishing – and why it is worth having – is difficult.

The Value of AmeriCorps

Since it was created twenty years ago, AmeriCorps has aimed to provide valuable services to communities, while also having a lifelong impact on the lives of its participants.

Some programs, such as Teach for America or the Harlem Children's Zone, have done this well. Participation in AmeriCorps has also left a lasting mark on many of its members, affecting their career plans as well as their involvement in civic life.[3]

But some programs have also had problems. Careful assessments have been few and those that were done often reached mixed conclusions.

Moreover, Americans do not look on serving one's country solely as a matter of participating in a government program, civilian or military. They embrace many other ways, not least of all volunteering. In 2013, nearly 63 million adults said they volunteered, including 6 percent who gave 500 hours or more, which is as much as some AmeriCorps members serve.

To deepen public support, AmeriCorps needs to draw on this tradition and reinforce it by giving its members a concentrated experience in citizenship. How it operates needs to be adjusted accordingly.

In other words, perhaps the time has come to stop thinking about AmeriCorps as "Swiss army knife," which can do all things for all people, and more as a classroom for democracy, which teaches the kinds of lessons the United States badly needs today. The stories in this volume make clear it is capable of doing so.

> " Participation in AmeriCorps has also left a lasting mark on many of its members, affecting their career plans as well as their involvement in civic life.[3] "

LESLIE LENKOWSKY is a Professor of Practice at the School of Public and Environmental Affairs and affiliated with the Lilly Family School of Philanthropy, Indiana University. From 2001 to 2003, he served as CEO of the Corporation for National and Community Service, after having previously served on its Board of Directors.

National Service Terms to Know

· ·

AmeriCorps- AmeriCorps engages more than 80,000 Americans in intensive service each year at nonprofits, schools, public agencies, and community and faith-based groups across the country. (http://www.nationalservice.gov/programs/americorps)

NCCC- AmeriCorps NCCC (National Civilian Community Corps) strengthens communities and develops leaders through direct, team-based national and community service. In partnership with non-profits—secular and faith based—local municipalities, state governments, federal government, national and state parks, Indian tribes, and schools, members complete service projects throughout the region they are assigned. AmeriCorps NCCC members serve for a 10-month commitment in teams of 8 to 12 and are assigned to projects throughout the region served by their campus. They are trained in CPR, first aid, public safety, and other skills before beginning their first service project. Members are based at one of five regional campuses and travel to complete service projects throughout those regions. (http://www.nationalservice.gov/programs/americorps/americorps-nccc)

VISTA- VISTA was founded as Volunteers in Service to America in 1965 as a national service program designed specifically to fight poverty in America. AmeriCorps VISTA members are passionate and committed to their mission to bring individuals and communities out of poverty.

Members make a year-long, full-time commitment to serve on a specific project at a nonprofit organization or public agency. They focus their efforts to build the organizational, administrative, and financial capacity of organizations that fight illiteracy, improve health services, foster economic development, and otherwise assist low-income communities. (http://www.nationalservice.gov/programs/americorps/americorps-vista)

State and National- AmeriCorps State and National supports a wide range of local service programs that engage thousands of Americans in intensive community service each year. Grants are given to a network of local and national organizations and agencies committed to using national service to address critical community needs in education, public safety, health, and the environment. (http://www.nationalservice.gov/programs/americorps/americorps-state-and-national)

SeniorCorps- Senior Corps connects today's 55+ with the people and organizations that need them most. Members become mentors, coaches or companions to people in need, or contribute their job skills and expertise to community projects and organizations. Volunteers receive guidance and training so they can make a contribution that suits their talents, interests, and availability. (http://www.nationalservice.gov/programs/senior-corps)

Foster Grandparent Program- Foster Grandparents are role models, mentors, and friends to children with exceptional needs. The program provides a way for volunteers age 55 and over to stay active by serving children and youth in their communities. Volunteers serve at thousands of local organizations that: help children learn to read and provide one-on-one tutoring, mentor troubled teenagers and young mothers, care for premature infants or children with disabilities, and help children who have been abused or neglected. (http://www.nationalservice.gov/programs/senior-corps/foster-grandparents)

Teach for America- TFA is a national teacher corps of college graduates and professionals who commit to teach for two years and raise student achievement in public schools.
(http://www.teachforamerica.org)

City Year- City Year is a proud member of the AmeriCorps network. This organization works to bridge the gap in high-poverty communities between the support that students actually need, and what their schools are designed and resourced to provide. In doing so, they're helping to increase graduation rates across the country.
(http://www.cityyear.org/about-us)

Public Allies- The Public Allies signature AmeriCorps Ally Program identifies diverse young adults and prepares them for leadership through paid full-time nonprofit apprenticeships and rigorous leadership training. Public Allies' mission is to advance new leadership to strengthen communities, nonprofits and civic participation. Public Allies is changing the face and practice of leadership in communities across the country by demonstrating the conviction that everyone can lead, and that lasting social change results when citizens of all backgrounds step up, take responsibility, and work together.
(http://www.publicallies.org/site/c.liKUL3PNLvF/b.2775807/k.C8B5/About_Us.htm)

Service as Legacy

By **Rachel Ogorek**

Served in AmeriCorps State and National with Community
Building Partnerships for Youth in Transition at the YMCA
Community Programs Branch at Bruce Randolph School
Denver, Colorado

I sat in the driver's seat. My car was packed to the brim with the exception of the passenger's seat, which would soon be occupied by my mother. Panic started to wash over me. I started to think of all of the things that could go wrong. What if I hated Denver? What if I did not make any friends? What if my new roommates were terrible? What if my job was awful? What if I loathed AmeriCorps? How was I possibly going to survive on the small living stipend? On and on my thoughts raged.

The passenger door opened and my mom stepped in. "Ready to go?"

"Mom, what am I doing? I can't pack up my life and move to Denver! I've never been there. I know no one. I will be all by myself. How could you let me make this decision?"

I was about to make the 1,100-mile journey to a new city, to live with two complete strangers, and work in an environment that was absolutely foreign to me. I was terrified of what was ahead. At the time, I was a recent college graduate who struggled for months to figure out the next step. I finished school in the midst of a national crisis— an economic recession. I was working part-time, but I was unable to find work that afforded me rewarding opportunities that would greatly benefit my personal and professional development.

In the midst of this struggle, I learned about AmeriCorps. I researched the organization and was impressed by the wide range of work the organization accomplished and the immense quantity of social justice issues AmeriCorps sought to address. There were a number of programs I found fascinating. The non-profit sector always intrigued me and AmeriCorps provided a way to gain valuable experience in the fields of social justice and philanthropy.

It was February when I started looking into AmeriCorps positions. I had committed my summer to working as a camp counselor in the wilderness and wanted to have an AmeriCorps position before I left in June. I spent months applying to various programs and decided to focus on seeking opportunities in places where I had connections. At the time, I was apprehensive about being alone. I had friends and family around the country; I thought surely I would have no problem finding a program near someone I already knew. I sent my resume and application to many programs of interest. I searched the AmeriCorps website daily for new job postings. I received returned calls but still no job offers.

> Literacy, math skills and passing grades are all important proficiencies. Students need these things to have success in the future. But students also need things like character, compassion, empathy, and the belief that they can be responsible citizens in their community.

As my departure date for camp quickly approached, I was still technically unemployed. I felt discouraged. Three weeks before my appointed camp date, my mother traveled to Denver, Colorado. While there, she called me and encouraged me to apply for programs in Denver. She fell in love with the entire city, and she knew the community and natural environment would be something I would appreciate and love as well.

I was skeptical at first, but I began to search for positions in Denver. The first AmeriCorps program that caught my attention was the Community Building Partnerships for Youth in Transition (CBPYT); it was located in the Denver Department of Human Services Building. This particular program worked with 15-20 organizations in Denver that specifically focused on transitioning youth. Each corps member was contracted out to an organization to help them with their mission. Corps members worked with students, refugees, teen parents, homeless youth, foster care youth and youth in transitional housing units. I was captivated with the program description and applied immediately. Within five days I was hired as a corps member.

After being hired by CBPYT, I had one more hurdle to jump through. I needed to be accepted and placed at a site; I chose three separate organizations for an interview. The YMCA Community Programs Branch stood out the most. For me, the YMCA Community Programs Branch was a new way of looking at community work. They were physically located at the school and offered a number of programs for students and their families, including after school programs, English language classes, and family nights. The Bruce Randolph School was in an urban setting that included grades 6-12 ranging from preteens to teenagers. Originally, this school was a poor performing school but had recently been reopened. The school was consistently graduating over 95% of its students.

Prior to my position, I was unfamiliar with public education. I was overwhelmed by all of the need as well as the opportunities that presented themselves as ways for me to be utilized in the school. Like many new things, it took some time for me to figure out the best way to become involved. Because the program offerings of the YMCA were so diverse, there were a number of ways my time and energy could have been used. My supervisors were patient as I explored the role I wanted to take. I was challenged to consider what I could contribute to the students, school and community. What could I do to maximize time and service for those around me?

As I dove into my work, many of the students became curious about AmeriCorps. What was it? Why did I want to volunteer? Wasn't volunteering usually a punishment? I saw the students' interest in the work as an opportunity to show the importance of giving back to their community. I wanted to show them that they had the power to change things they found disagreeable in their community. They were just as capable as anyone to address some of the needs in their neighborhood. I wanted to find a way to impact the school as a whole, so I decided to create a community day of service involving the entire high school student body.

This task was no small feat. I needed to secure food, transportation and organizations with which to partner; not to mention, convincing my site supervisor, AmeriCorps supervisor, school staff and the teachers that this was a meaningful and valuable investment for the students and for their community. Some people were initially hesitant to devote a whole day out of the classroom to community service. Many of their fears were valid; there is a lot of pressure on teachers to produce results. Time spent outside of the classroom takes away from instructional time. I was slightly discouraged, but these concerns allowed for a larger conversation to take place.

Several staff were open to the discussion that we go back to the basics and consider what it means to be educated. Literacy, math skills and passing grades are all important proficiencies. Students need these things to have success in the future. But students also need things like character, compassion, empathy, and the belief that they can be responsible citizens in their community. Schools can't create these things from scratch, nor is that their role, but they can aid in the development of these behaviors. Service and community awareness are great ways to accomplish this. This discussion breathed new life into the service project.

Once everyone was on board, many people became excited about the day. There was a lot of support, but not many resources for this kind of project. I spent months networking in Denver and bothering friends and family back home begging them for donations and monetary support. There are costs associated with transporting, feeding, and taking care of hundreds of people. Even as I was working on the costs and logistics of the project, I started to brainstorm ways to market this idea to the students and the community. What should we call this day? I learned the school was named after a strong community leader, Bruce Randolph. This man managed a local BBQ restaurant and every Thanksgiving donated food to disadvantaged families in the neighborhood around the school. Bruce Randolph has since passed away, but his work and legacy live on to this day. Every Thanksgiving food baskets continue to be given away in his honor.

Since childhood, I too have been captivated by the idea of leaving a legacy. My parents instilled this in me from a young age. No one is too small to affect things they want to see changed. I decided to call the service day "Students in Action: Continuing the Legacy". I wanted students to continue the legacy Bruce Randolph began in the community. I hoped this service day would help show them they are just as capable as Randolph to create change while serving others.

On Friday, April 29, 2011, the first annual Students in Action Service Day launched. Approximately 550 students, teachers, staff, AmeriCorps members and community volunteers went into the Denver Metro Area to complete various service projects. We partnered with five Denver organizations and contributed approximately 2,200 volunteer hours of service. The service day tide started to roll! I knew I wanted to sign on for a second year of AmeriCorps to continue expanding and developing the project. My AmeriCorps supervisor and site supervisor inspired me to develop the work. How could I get more students involved? What other organizations would consider partnering? How could students take a bigger role in planning the day?

> My life is imprinted forever because of the friendships I made, relationships I formed and experiences I was given.

The following school year I started a student volunteer club. We volunteered twice a month at various organizations and with diverse challenges around Denver. I wanted students to see new opportunities in their own backyard. I asked what they wanted to learn more about and sought organizations where they could experience these things for themselves. We visited Veterans at the VA hospital, prepared a meal for homeless youth, wrapped Christmas presents for seniors at the Salvation Army, cleaned graffiti off playsets in their neighborhood parks, and many other projects. As the student group gained momentum, we started to look for ways to expand the successful work from the previous year during the school wide service day.

As the second annual Students in Action Service Day dawned, twelve other nearby schools in Denver joined us. More than 4,000 people went out and served in 25 non-profit organizations. The community received approximately 12,000 volunteer hours during this one-day event. The substantial growth in one year showed effectual change was happening within the school and within the community. The first year it was challenging to find organizations to take on busloads of students and there were not as many resources available. The second year organizations were calling me to see if the service day was happening again and if they could partner with the school. One organization, Challenge Denver, offered substantial financial support to ensure we had all of the resources we needed to make this day a success.

> "Not only do I believe in the legacy individuals can leave, but I believe in the legacy of AmeriCorps. It is no small thing to believe national service can change the course of an individual life, a school, a neighborhood, a community, a city, a state, a region and a nation."

The greatest change took place within the student body. The first year, a minority group of students skipped the service day because they did not want to participate. Many of those students were present for the second service day knowing they had missed out on an opportunity. One of the students who skipped the first day became a champion of service the second year. She was active in the student volunteer club and in the Students in Action Day. She had this to say about service: "Volunteering has introduced me to problems in my community and opened my eyes to the fact that we all must take responsibility in helping others. Several service projects have taught me to be more compassionate and have given me a desire to teach my fellow classmates to be part of positive community changes."

Another student experienced a large personal change that shaped her educational and career path. This student was a senior during the first Students in Action day and she was struggling with her post high school plans. The service project she participated in took place at a large urban farm in Denver. During the course of the day, she learned about all of the internships and other volunteer options the farm provided during after school and summer hours. This student applied for a paid intensive summer internship that explored things like urban farming, food justice, food deserts and access to healthy food. Through that internship, the student received a scholarship to a local community college that allowed her to continue her internship, while pursuing a higher education degree in nutrition and teaching. She is passionate about food justice and community building and is studying to become a teacher. Her goal is to come back to the neighborhood to teach local school children the importance of good nutrition.

These changes, along with countless others, are continual reminders of how grateful I am for the experience of AmeriCorps and for the things I learned over the course of my two-year term. A year has passed since the last service project and I have spent time reflecting on how my thinking has expanded. My life is imprinted forever because of the friendships I made, relationships I formed and experiences I was given. As I move on to graduate school and eventually a career, the question my parents etched in my heart and AmeriCorps confirmed still remains, "What kind of legacy do I want to leave?"

This question inspired me to write my own story and to compel others to share their experiences to compile this book. Not only do I believe in the legacy individuals can leave, but I believe in the legacy of AmeriCorps. It is no small thing to believe national service can change the course of an individual life, a school, a neighborhood, a community, a city, a state, a region and a nation. AmeriCorps provides individuals the opportunity to serve, but its reach is far greater because it instills a "pay-it-forward" mentality among individuals to keep the flow going indefinitely. Throughout my own service, I witnessed exemplary service by creating opportunities for others to provide service. This has the power to change the trajectory of communities by impacting individual lives. It is the power of AmeriCorps; this is the legacy it leaves.

> "Throughout my own service, I witnessed exemplary service by creating opportunities for others to provide service. This has the power to change the trajectory of communities by impacting individual lives.

RACHEL OGOREK is currently putting her education award to good use by pursuing her Masters in Public Administration in Nonprofit Management at the School of Public and Environmental Affairs as well as her Masters in Philanthropy at the Indiana University Lilly School of Philanthropy.

AmeriCorps: Looking Outward, Inward, Forward

By Nicole Vera

Served in AmeriCorps State and National with Community
Building Partnerships for Youth in Transition
Denver, Colorado

It's winter in Kansas and I-70 seems flatter than usual. The fields are dry, no clouds in sight, and the few trees here are, for the most part, bare. This is my fourth time crossing the Sunflower State and each time it's a reflective process. For a lot of people, crossing Kansas means trying to attain the ever-allusive sweet spot of avoiding the state patrol and pushing 85mph. I'm not immune to the temptation—alas, my last speeding ticket was in Kansas. But as I'm sitting in the passenger seat of a Budget moving truck, I'm comparing Toto's homeland to the *Meseta*, a roughly 100-mile stretch of flat, straight path on the Camino de Santiago in Spain. The Camino de Santiago, more affectionately known as The Camino, is a 2,000 year old pilgrimage roughly 500 miles long from the French-Spanish border to Santiago de Compostela in Western Spain. As a pilgrim, walking the Camino is done in three phases: looking outward, looking inward, and looking forward. The *Meseta* is arguably the most important phase on the pilgrimage, it's a time to look inward and right now, Kansas is my Meseta. But, let's start at the beginning…

-looking outward-

I'm remembering the last 5 years: moving to Colorado to serve in AmeriCorps, becoming an AmeriCorps Program Manager, and quitting my job to take my love of service around the world. My service story starts with an adventure and a gamble to quit a job in D.C. and flee to the Rockies to join AmeriCorps. Like many alums, I can attest that AmeriCorps changed my life—and continues to. Four years in the "Ameri-world" created the perfect storm: enough civic activity and reflection to propel me forward to global servitude. By September 2012, I left AmeriCorps Management to volunteer with a small non-profit in Peru's Sacred Valley, aptly named the Sacred Valley Project. My husband, Sean—also an AC Alum—and I spent six months working with (but mostly learning from) adolescent girls from rural, highland communities. I tutored, taught life-skill classes, visited communities, developed a service project, and on occasion, cut and washed hair. More than that, the girls and staff from the Sacred Valley Project became family.

If you're wondering how on Earth my husband, Sean and I were able to do this, you aren't the first. Peru was an easy choice because I'm half Peruvian—so that crossed out 195 other countries. Though what really made this come together, was looking outward: to our friends, families, communities, and networks. It happened that two of our friends were already deeply tied to the Sacred Valley Project and as our friendships grew, so did the amount of Peru-themed conversations, held over copious amounts of wine. These conversations ultimately led to resignations and one-way plane tickets.

> It helped me to live simply and slow down long enough to look outward and build community.

As for the financial side of things, and aside from the obvious "put your money under the mattress" advice, we knew we were making a decision to live simply, not just for the year we were gone, but also for the foreseeable future. To us, it was worth it.

On a side note: we also sought out volunteer opportunities with small non-profits or organizations that did not have formal volunteer programs so as to avoid any and all pay-to-volunteer experiences.

-looking inward-

> Without my AmeriCorps experience I never would have done this trip, or at the very least I wouldn't have done it so successfully—not to say, I didn't make mistakes, have lots of illnesses, bugs, you name it.

Once the rains let up in Peru, we made our way to Spain to walk the Camino. We started in St. Jean Pied de Port, France on May 8, not knowing anyone and barely able to say *Bonjour*. As we crossed the Pyrenees with hundreds of other pilgrims, thoughts of Peru would not leave me. After all, I was leaving the land of the conquered for the land of the conquerors and the juxtaposition was startling. Reminding myself to look outward, I put those thoughts to rest (or at least, on hold) so I could meet my new community: my fellow pilgrims. Along the way, Sean and I befriended an Opera singer, a witch, a minister, an ex-nun, a surfer, a blind man and his dog, and a nurse. Being a part of this eclectic community kept me going, especially in moments when I was forced to joyfully rely on friends.

The *Meseta* is not only a straight path with mostly flat terrain, it's the sunniest—and the windiest. As we set off in the mornings, the Sun lay to the east, causing our bodies to cast our shadows to the West, making it seem as if we were walking straight into our pasts... or our futures. Yes, the time for introspection had arrived and my shadow was the perfect conduit for reflection and deep philosophizing. After days on the *Meseta*, we found ourselves looking forward not just as solitary, individual pilgrims but as a community of pilgrims. The excitement was palpable but we didn't hurry, we enjoyed the stroll through Spain and knew arrival to Santiago de Compostela was not the real end, anyway. We were looking forward to our lives beyond Santiago.

-looking forward-

Beyond Santiago lay more volunteering—this time in Africa. We chose Africa for two reasons: 1) it was the furthest place outside our comfort zones and 2) Paul Simon's musical prowess. A month after the Camino we found ourselves in Geita, Tanzania. Much like Peru, our connection to Tanzania came through community. We happened to meet a Tanzanian Catholic Priest who invited us to volunteer and we spent months Skyping with him to prepare for our visit and the work we'd be doing. Sean is an AmeriCorps Alum with Habitat for Humanity who turned Civil Engineer. He designed a new school and I worked at an orphanage. Our hosts were gracious enough to house and feed us during our volunteer work, but most gracious of all was welcoming us into their community.

> "AmeriCorps inspired me to test the waters, confront my fears, and push the boundaries of my comfort zone—to look forward to what I can do and who I can become."

Geita is a small gold mining town near Mwanza, a city on the shores of Lake Victoria. It's an arduous journey to Gieta involving two plane rides, a boat ride, and a drive, leaving it well off the beaten path for tourists. Unfortunately, the gold mine and the International roadway that travels through Geita to Uganda, Rwanda, and Burundi have unintentionally created an industry for trafficking and prostitution, making it an area with a high rate of HIV-AIDS. The orphanage exists to care for children affected by HIV-AIDS. My days consisted of teaching classes (or trying to), cooking, gardening, cleaning, and playing games with the kids.

The experience was like that in Peru—I learned more than I taught. Like anything, it wasn't without its mishaps; I fainted at a hospital and became the spectacle white woman, who upon regaining consciousness vomited in front of everyone in the Malaria-test line. Even so, Tanzania was the hardest place to leave. It was the country in which I learned the most because I was so far outside of my comfort zone with the language and the culture. I also had a fear of the unknown: Geita, and the surrounding bush villages were the most remote places I had ever visited.

Without my AmeriCorps experience I never would have done this trip, or at the very least I wouldn't have done it so successfully—not to say, I didn't make mistakes, have lots of illnesses, bugs, you name it. Yet AmeriCorps had prepared me to be flexible, adaptive, and patient during the normal occurrences of working and living in a developing country. We encountered anything from unreliable electricity to extraordinary delays. It helped me to live simply and slow down long enough to look outward and build community. AmeriCorps made me more culturally sensitive and aware, by forcing me to look inward to acknowledge my sense of entitlement and privilege and in doing so, allowing me to approach service and volunteerism as a learner rather than a teacher, a helper, or a fixer. AmeriCorps inspired me to test the waters, confront my fears, and push the boundaries of my comfort zone—to look forward to what I can do and who I can become.

NICOLE VERA is currently an AmeriCorps Program Manager at Reading Partners, a national education nonprofit focused on increasing literacy skills among elementary school students from low income communities. She continues to volunteer with the Sacred Valley Project, a nonprofit dedicated to improving access to education for young women from low-income families in remote, mountain communities of Peru's Sacred Valley. More of her writing can be found at servingforward.tumblr.com.

Choosing Love First

By **Anna Lenhart**

* Names have been changed
** Contains some strong language

Served as a VISTA at Shakti Rising
San Diego, California

From my office on the first floor of a Victorian-styled home, lovingly referred to as the "Sunshine House" I heard the crash and yelling, "I fucking hate you!" I was downstairs developing technology applications to support a non-profit called Shakti Rising's. Kaylin, a recovering heroin addict, had just flipped the desk of my co-worker during an aggressive nervous breakdown. I ran up to the office, though at a mere 105 pounds I'm not sure what I intended to do. All I knew was that I loved both of these young women, and that Kaylin's aggression stemmed from fear that emerges with sobriety after 6 years of numbness. She needed to feel loved. So that is what I did; that is what *we* did. It was the first line of the Shakti Rising's value statement: *"We are a vibrant, eclectic community of individuals, who recognize interconnectedness, believe in goodness, choose love first."*

These incidents were not infrequent during the year I spent as an AmeriCorps VISTA at Shakti Rising, a woman's recovery home and empowerment program in San Diego. Ironically, it was my own

> " All I knew was that I loved both of these young women, and that Kaylin's aggression stemmed from fear that emerges with sobriety after 6 years of numbness. "

mild breakdown that led me to take a leave of absence from Carnegie Mellon University, where I was pursuing an engineering degree, and move to California.

In high school, I became accustomed to winning, on the sports field, in student government elections, and in the classroom. This was not the case at Carnegie Mellon where I began to feel small, worthless and anxious. The anxiety brought about an array of health problems: rapid weight loss, insomnia, and shortness of breath. My life was becoming a list of side effects at the end of a commercial for pharmaceutical drugs. I needed to feel valued. In high school, I had been actively involved in Kiwanis and 4-H. I had served soup to the homeless, painted houses for Habitat for Humanity and organized clothing drives- simple things that looked good on a college application, but provided so much more than a strong resume. At Carnegie Mellon, in the midst of learning C++ and how to design bridges that could withstand a hurricane, I yearned to feel that same sense of meaning and purpose I had experienced while doing service. I decided to take a leave of absence to participate in AmeriCorps. My mentors frowned upon the idea of leaving school, but the decline in my health signaled to me that I needed the healing that occurs as a result of giving oneself to a cause.

At my first staff meeting on my first day at Shakti Rising, I sat on the side of the room as staff crowded in at a round table. Before I could get comfortable, the Director of Education and Community Wellness turned to me and said, "Everyone in this organization sits at the table." It was clear I would be treated as a leader, regardless of my position as a volunteer and this "year off" was really a "year on."

During the third week, while I was helping write grants and getting to know the women in the program, Shakti Rising's website was infected with a virus and needed to be taken down immediately. All the files were destroyed, and as the token "techie" on staff, I felt responsible to remedy the situation. With little programming experience (I had built one incredibly basic HTML website before this project), I worked closely with the designer, an apprentice, who was also a woman in Shakti Rising's intensive recovery program. For all other questions, I leaned on volunteers in the community and the Google search engine. I was able to get the site up in one 90-hour work-week. This was not my first 90-hour work-week, but it was the first one fueled by a mission of social change. There were no "A's" awarded, no prize money involved, just all the women on the edge of relapse sitting in front of computers searching for help from our website.

It was during this project my relationship with work changed. From that point forward, I knew I wanted to live a mission-driven life, where personal self and work are no longer separate entities, but fuelled by a passion to improve lives.

> this "year off" was really a "year on."

I spent the remainder of service bringing technological solutions to the organization's programs. My largest contribution was to develop a web-based client relations management (CRM) system to track volunteers, donors, students, and women in our intensive recovery program. The organization is still using the CRM and other web applications I created to grow and sustain themselves. The mark I left on the organization, however, cannot compare to the mark it left on me.

Working with women who have suffered abuse, loss, and rejection beyond my experience, caused a shift in perspective. The fear of getting a "B" or not having the most prestigious job of all my classmates was replaced with a drive to make a difference and inspire others to do the same. I began to understand hard times in life made me more open to give and receive love; and acting from a place of compassion was more important than winning.

The life-threatening challenges women in our program face are rooted in the same fundamental issue underlying my anxiety: not feeling loved for who I am as a person. Recognizing this connection transformed me into an empathetic leader and allowed me to heal alongside the apprentices at Shakti Rising.

I ended my year as a VISTA understanding that answers to the world's problems lie in people connecting to their calling and living in a community that *chooses love first*.

I returned to Carnegie Mellon to complete my degree in engineering with a different perspective and a goal of exploring my life calling. As my peers and I began the quest of "finding a job", it was impossible not to be discouraged by the options. It seemed that in a world with wars over oil, extreme poverty juxtaposed with extreme wealth, and the rising occurrence of depression, the only companies recruiting were the ones who created these problems in the first place. Where were organizations with a mission to change the world?

I spent time in between cover letters and career fairs reflecting on how easy it would be to take a typical engineering job if I had never enrolled in AmeriCorps. I would be less civically engaged and less entrepreneurial. Now all I could think about was making change either inside industry, through academia, or in the social sector, and I knew I was not alone. There were other people who wanted to make a difference in their careers, but lacked an opportunity, a window to explore things that excite and energize them, issues that stir and enrage them. I began encouraging my peers to participate in national service. I explained that being out of their comfort zones would prompt personal reflection; working with underserved populations would spark their interest in social issues. All these things would better equip them to create change in their future line of work, or better yet, create business not solely driven by huge profit margins.

I loved the way this sort of "alternative career counseling" made me feel. It happened effortlessly and gave me energy, and in all conversations with young people it was clear this sort of counseling was necessary. I decided to start an organization that pairs mentors with students who want to make a difference but are unsure of how to proceed. The mentors offer resources to help students uncover their passion and encourage them to participate in or create a stipend service year program. The organization is called the NGS (Next Generation of Service) Movement.

When deciding where to launch the NGS Movement, I felt called to return to the community of change makers I belonged to in San Diego. With support from my friends at Shakti Rising and integrating what I had learned in regards to empowerment, I began recruiting people who have participated in national service to serve as mentors. We began working with students at the University of San Diego and are now replicating the program in other universities nationwide. The experience has instilled in me excitement for the impact our generation will have and the legacy they will leave.

Most importantly I live my life differently now, not for vain accomplishment but for whatever I am called to do in the world. I am slowly learning to surrender to the journey that will define my life. I'm learning to trust when things do not go the way I planned; taking time to reflect and remember.

Kaylin's journey as a Shakti Rising apprentice ended a year ago when she graduated from the program. She is currently studying nutrition and volunteering at Shakti Rising, providing support to women in the apprenticeship program. One evening last fall, Beth, a current apprentice struggling with alcoholism and suicidal thoughts, left her therapy session sobbing and angry. She ran out of the house to her car fuming. Recognizing that Beth was a danger to herself and others, Kaylin chased after her. As Beth began to drive away, Kaylin jumped on the hood of Beth's car forcing her to stop. Kaylin remained sprawled out on the hood of the car for an hour while staff proceeded to calm Beth down and coax her to pull over and park. Later that night when Beth expressed her embarrassment over the episode, Kaylin

> " I ended my year as a VISTA understanding that answers to the world's problems lie in people connecting to their calling and living in a community that *chooses love first.* "

and I looked at each other, grinned, and began reminiscing about our early days in recovery. Sometimes breakdowns are necessary catalysts for growth, and when they happen in a community that chooses love first, they can (and in my experience often do) lead to breakthrough.

ANNA LENHART is the Founder of the Next Generation of Service, which connects young people to social change organizations by offering vocational mentorship and promoting community and international service as a component of any career path. Learn more about becoming a mentor or receiving guidance at www.ngsmovement.org.

Consider the Ripples

By Blake Shultice

*Names have been changed

State & National AmeriCorps with Cispus
Educational Center & Teach for America
Randle, Washington, & Milwaukee, Wisconsin

hen I graduated from college in May of 2011, I was an archetype of the ambitious, idealistic, confused, and overwhelmed student entering the working world. I had a degree in economics, which had been a part of the original plan, and I also had one in philosophy, which had not been. I benefited from the aggressive recruiting efforts of the humanities program and one professor in particular convinced me to welcome modern ethicists into my life (the dead white guys then followed suit). I became another cross-disciplinary graduate of Simpson College, a small liberal arts school outside of Des Moines.

Degree in hand, I faced the paradox of choice that challenges millions of modern college graduates—more social and economic mobility than ever before, but no obvious path. I could have found a job with an insurance company in Des Moines and embraced its career trajectory, but such options didn't personally resonate with me. In my last few years at Simpson I had brushed shoulders with people who were involved in innovative and impactful NGO work in the area, be it urban farming initiatives (like the wonderful Des Moines farmers market), after-school tutoring for at-risk urban youth, or Habitat for Humanity's tangible work to provide access to quality housing. I dabbled in some of these efforts myself on a volunteer basis, but I found no immediate prospects for employment post-graduation in central Iowa. And elsewhere? Again, where should one even begin looking? I felt paralyzed by having 15,000 interests but few specialized, marketable skills that would give me any sort of niche advantage.

Enter national civil service. Or rather, first enter my then-girlfriend- and now wife- Andrea. It was to my heart's chagrin that she graduated a year before me and moved to Denver to volunteer with AmeriCorps. My sentiment towards this decision on her part softened considerably as I learned more about the wonderful work she was doing with foster youth through Denver's Department of Human Services office. This exposure to full time national service quickly kindled my own interest in such an endeavor.

My efforts to join Andrea in Denver with an AmeriCorps position didn't pan out, but my own opportunity materialized farther west. Four months after graduation, I found myself in Randle, Washington, an unincorporated outpost nestled between three volcanic giants: Mt. Rainier, Mt. St. Helens, and Mt. Adams. Randle is a logging town, not unlike myriad others in the Pacific Northwest, and like most it has clung to life for several decades now, rooted in blue collar industry and plagued by the same globalization-era struggles that are shared elsewhere. It was also home to the Cispus educational center, which operated a small AmeriCorps program that spanned three small school districts in the sparsely populated Cowlitz valley.

The fact that formal opportunities in national service are available in barely-on-the-map places like Randle is a strong testament to its reach and its potential for a great personal fit. With AmeriCorps, candidates seek out and apply for specific positions that appeal to them based on the type of work and its context. In Washington alone, AmeriCorps jobs varied from educational volunteers in the heart of Seattle, to trail crews deep in the pristine forests of the North Cascades. The fact that people have the chance to choose a workspace that is or is not a thriving grizzly bear habitat, speaks to the accessibility and appeal of AmeriCorps.

My particular job found me in a few different capacities. In Randle's

White Pass elementary school, I was an intervention tutor four days a week, helping kindergarteners master the hard "K" sound one minute and then helping fifth graders with social studies homework the next. I also co-ran a recreational after-school program in nearby Packwood, also a part of White Pass schools. Two nights a week we offered a space for local kids to play basketball, make crafts, and get homework help as needed. We also organized field trips, giving many of our youth their first brush with professional baseball, an ocean beach, or Mt. Rainier National Park. Beyond these two places, auxiliary responsibilities involved helping one of my 11 coworkers with their own work, hosting parents' night at Mossyrock school district for Spanish-speaking parents or helping with a clothing drive in Morton.

For me, national service was a place where many fragmented ideas, values, and interests found concrete footing. I learned much about balancing human needs with ecological well-being while living in the mountains. Randle sat at a confluence of privately owned land, national forests, and the nearby national park; all representing vastly different philosophies and practices for land stewardship. I learned about the struggles of people in such areas to find sustainable employment, secure access to healthy food and medical services, and be recognized and represented by the political powers in state and federal government. I also learned poignant lessons about educational inequities in many rural communities through the students I worked with and the educators who labored to do the best they could with limited resources in a difficult setting.

Of course, one of the critical questions on the value of national service is whether the efforts expended have measurable, impactful benefits on the communities they aim to serve. A typical question would be: the majority of civil service volunteers are only freshly removed from undergraduate lives, filled with idealistic boldness but lacking a nuanced perspective and wisdom of the great and diverse world. Can idealistic undergraduates have enough wisdom and perspective to impact the world or was my time spent in national service a thinly veiled pursuit of a great resume item and/or a self-centered journey of adventurous dabbling and soul-searching as opposed to an authentic commitment to serving others?

I wrestled with these concerns often when I was in Washington, and I continue to since leaving (after one year I took a different position in Milwaukee, which further fans the "is it genuine service?" fire). Biased as I might be towards validating my own work, my belief in my specific opportunity, and in national service as a worthwhile institution, has grown. I mentioned earlier that abstract notions were given concrete traction. This happened most profoundly through specific people my program served. One boy in particular—I'll call him Michael—will always be the first one to come back to my mind. He was in the first grade for the second time, having been retained due to his struggles with reading. His home was marred with the devastating effects of substance abuse, and he often came to school bearing indications he wasn't rested, clean, or, quite simply, loved the way a young child should be. And yet he had an incredibly kind and sensitive heart, and he had an inner fire that burned bright. He wanted to read. He *passionately* wanted to read. He just needed someone to spend time one-on-one with him reinforcing skills most of his first grade peers had already mastered. And that's where I—Mr. Blake—could help.

Every day Michael excitedly grabbed his intervention reading materials and led the way down the hallway to our workspace. There he enthusiastically and methodically learned to read. The rapidity with which improvements came astounded me, and the chart where he graphed his progress became a treasured object. It was usually clutched tightly in his hands as he showed it off to yet another teacher in the school. By the end of the year he had made enormous strides towards being on track with his peers. When I knew with certainty I wasn't returning to the program the following year, his teacher assuaged my worries about Michael's future (and, more selfishly, about me missing him and him potentially forgetting me). "You taught him to read," said the other teacher "and he won't forget that. Nor will he forget you. And he certainly isn't going to stop reading".

> I don't remember when I first entertained the notion of teaching as a vocation, nor when I decided to pursue it, but this development was manifested through my work in Washington.

I believe that my work with Michael impacted his future trajectory. In a school with limited resources, there were no conventional staff members who could devote significant one-on-one time to him every single day, even though it was unequivocally clear this was what he needed. My position allowed it to happen. Michael is going to succeed and be happy in life, primarily because he has a great heart and an incredible will to succeed. However, I think the boost I was able to give him came at a vital, formative time in his life. He is still swimming against a difficult current, but I think he will succeed.

I had such a rewarding opportunity at White Pass Elementary to work with students who needed crucial bits of extra support. I spent a lot of time with Haley, another first grader, who was struggling with subtraction. We practiced with cubes and fingers for many, many weeks until she got the hang of it. I also got to know a sixth grader named Bobby who needed an ally. His outward apathy towards school masked internal insecurities. I worked to build his confidence, be a confidant, and try to prepare him for the leap to middle school the following year. I also tried to help him organize his desk. Unfortunately this project has to be recorded as a failure. Essentially, without the full responsibilities of formal teachers, I was able to provide interventions wherever and whenever needed.

~

I don't remember when I first entertained the notion of teaching as a vocation, nor when I decided to pursue it, but this development was manifested through my work in Washington. Lacking an undergraduate degree in education, I could have gone back to school. The reality was I had no desire to spend the time nor money doing so. I thus turned to fellowship programs as an option for an immediate transition into teaching and was led to Teach for America. As an alternative licensure program, TFA accepts "corps members" who haven't formally studied education. We all receive an intensive summer training and short student teaching stint. Afterward, we're placed in low-income schools in one of dozens of regions around the country. I got sent to Milwaukee.

Standing in front of a classroom after just a few whirlwind months of crash-course prep was the most surreal experience of my life. And it was terrifying. Absolutely terrifying. I kept expecting someone important- my principal, someone from the Department of Education- to burst through the door and drag me out as a teaching quack; someone who surely was not yet fit to lead a class of living, breathing students. I felt that 25 years working as a tutor at White Pass would not have helped me avoid acute anxiety about the entire situation. As days, weeks, and months passed, the realization slowly settled in; I truly was a *teacher*. Someone did charge me with teaching students in my room and I might survive the experience.

> It allowed me to meet and work with immensely wonderful young people. Their triumphs and joys warmed my heart, their sorrows broke it, their behavior very often stressed it, but ultimately won it.

I think it's safe to say Teach for America makes a great post-AmeriCorps chapter in itself, indicating that AmeriCorps changed the course of my vocational journey. But it's even better: TFA is partially funded by AmeriCorps. National Service directly enabled the leap I made to work more closely with students who need a quality education. It allowed me to meet and work with immensely wonderful young people. Their triumphs and joys warmed my heart, their sorrows broke it, their behavior very often stressed it, but ultimately won it. It has been such a trying, joyful, terrifying, and rewarding chapter in my life. AmeriCorps further solidified my desire to build a vocation out of teaching. It furthered my conviction that I could make ripples of change through education. This fall, in my third year in the classroom, I'll continue to build on the foundation National Service helped build.

~

Before Andrea departed for her work in Denver, one of our mutual friends told her the key to fighting the good fight in the social services field was to realize this: social workers might see very few indications their work is resulting in positive outcomes. The outcomes they help bring about often transpire by long series of events; ripples are still effecting change long after the social worker might be out of the picture. I have considered this advice often. I was lucky enough to get to see Michael make considerable academic gains, but he still has a long route in front of him. If I were forced to stand before a congressional budget committee and prove the impact of my program on the Cowlitz River valley was worth the investment, it would be hard to do with numbers.

But I could ask them to consider the ripples.

BLAKE SHULTICE recently completed his second year of Teach for America at the Milwaukee Academy of Science in Wisconsin. In the fall of 2014, he will be teaching 4th grade in West Branch, Iowa.

Educating Beyond the Classroom

By Andalisa Lopez

Served as a Maryland DC Campus Compact
AmeriCorps VISTA at American University
Washington, DC

hen people hear "AmeriCorps" they probably picture someone helping in a school, working at a food bank, or with a hammer in hand building a family a home. I always love to hear about other AmeriCorps members' experiences building schools, teaching children, or creating community gardens. I think people are always a bit surprised to learn that I spent my AmeriCorps VISTA year at a university in Washington, DC. Not exactly a community "in need" you might think. So what kind of impact can an AmeriCorps member have at an institution of higher education?

Let's start at the beginning: I was one of those college students who stumbled into community service because, frankly, I needed an on campus job. I worked all four years at the college's Community Service Office both in an administrative capacity, but also as a mentor to community youth through a small nonprofit organization. Little did I know that my work with the community, and the office, would ignite a life-long passion for service.

As a college student, I volunteered in the surrounding community and each day I felt good about the work I was doing to impact young people of Allentown, PA. I relished in the chance to get off campus and into the community; it was refreshing to interact with people outside of the homogeneous population at school. I was not only volunteering in the community, but I was also working in the Office of Community Engagement on campus. Through my experience with the community service office, I took advantage of structured reflection times to think about the impact of service. As I reflected on my time spent in the community I began to realize how much volunteering actually benefited me personally: it was stress relieving to get off campus for a few hours each week to spend time with kids. On top of that, I was getting valuable experience, I was earning money—it was my job afterall—and I certainly got those warm fuzzies because I was "helping others". But what were the people I worked with getting out of this relationship? What impact was I really making in the community? I began to think about my service experiences with a critical lens, and began to ponder larger social justice issues that impacted the community.

> I began to think about my service experiences with a critical lens, and began to ponder larger social justice issues that impacted the community.

As graduation approached, pressure was on to figure out that next step. I knew I wanted to continue volunteering in some capacity and I wanted to continue to wrestle with these question, I also wanted to be in Washington, DC. When I heard about AmeriCorps, I knew that would be my next step.

> Service is about mutuality and reciprocity, and this is especially crucial in a university-community partnership.

When I took the pledge at the pre-service orientation, I was not just becoming an AmeriCorps member, or a VISTA, but I was walking across a bridge between higher education and service; I was becoming a member of the Campus Compact network. Officially, I was part of the Maryland DC Campus Compact and had to learn each time I introduced myself I would say "I am a Maryland DC Campus Compact AmeriCorps

VISTA…". It was a mouthful, but it was meaningful and differentiated my experience from many other AmeriCorps members I met along the way.

My AmeriCorps VISTA year brought me to a university in the nation's capital; I worked with college students at a center of service similar to the one I had worked at during my undergraduate career. As a VISTA, I would be supporting the day to day functions of the city-wide tutoring program while assessing the impact of the program from a variety of perspectives: that of the student tutors, the tutees, and the community partner. I was also helping to connect many philosophical academic subjects into real life tangible experiences for college students with whom I worked. Too often college students ignore or abuse the community in which they call their home for four years; they fail to see themselves as an important change agent and advocate in that community. Students rarely realize how valuable a resource a community can be throughout their four years of college. Many of the students I worked with wanted to pursue a career in education, so signing up to tutor children in DC offered them invaluable experience to document on their resume and discuss in job interviews.

> Education should be paired with experience, and this is part of why Campus Compact exists; it benefits both the students and the broader community. One should never be without the other.

While I was interacting with the college students, much of my time was spent trying to better understand the community partnership by talking one-on-one with our many partner programs. Service is about mutuality and reciprocity, and this is especially crucial in a university-community partnership. AmeriCorps is about building capacity, and in this particular case it was about leveraging university resources to boost the capacity of the community, and in return the students are able to grow and learn outside the classroom.

Education is about pushing boundaries, expanding the mind to other worlds and possibilities; it's about reaching beyond what you know and critically examining the world around you. You can also think of service in this vein as well. Education should be paired with experience, and this is part of why Campus Compact exists; it benefits both the students and the broader community. One should never be without the other. Together they can affect the world and bring about meaningful social change.

When I think back to my time at college, volunteering was just as valuable to my education as the course work. My experience in communities expanded my mind to consider other points of view and allowed me to contextualize my studies in a way that merely reading a book could not. My AmeriCorps VISTA year allowed me to share the impactful benefits of service with other college students. My year as a Campus Compact AmeriCorps VISTA allowed me to share the love of service with others. Together, our volunteers impacted hundreds of students throughout Washington, DC, and many college students with which I worked are now on track to become teachers who will continue to impact generations to come.

ANDALISA LOPEZ is continuing to pursue social justice at a national literacy organization in Washington, DC. She hopes to put her education award to good use in the near future and looks forward to building more bridges between education and service.

Mixing the Old with the New

· ·

By Dilli R Chapagai

Served in an AmeriCorps State Program
with the Power of We Consortium
Lansing, Michigan

A long Journey

I was born in Bhutan – a small mountainous country in South Asia that lies between two giant countries, China and India. The majority of the population in Bhutan practice Buddhism. However, other religions are practiced as well, including Hinduism. In the northern part of the country most of the population speaks the national and native language: Dzongkha, while Nepali speaking individuals occupy the southern part of the country.

Bhutanese of Nepali origin, in the southern part of the country, have their own language, culture, and clothing that is very different from the native Bhutanese population. The way the southern Bhutanese of Nepali origin came to be is quite complicated. What I have learned from my culture is that during the late 19th century our Nepali ancestors were brought to Bhutan by the government to start agriculture in the uninhabited southern areas. By the early 20th century, most of the southern parts of land in Bhutan were inhabited by the Bhutanese of Nepali origin.

During the time Bhutan became an agriculturally based country;

· · · · · · · ·

farming was the only way to sustain life in the southern region. Unfortunately, in 1990, around 70,000 - 80,000 Bhutanese of Nepali origin were evicted from their homeland. This happened for a number of reasons, but primarily because there was unrest among the Bhutanese of Nepali origin, who had begun to raise their voices because they wanted basic civil rights including freedom to practice their religion and free speech. My family was one family among the 80,000 individuals forced from their homes. During the 1990 insurgency, many innocent people were arrested, brutally tortured, and killed. Most of the people who were forced from their homes were coerced at gunpoint into signing forms stating they were leaving the country by their own freewill.

> When I was young, I was fascinated by all of the help I received from various agencies while I was in the refugee camp. I thought of this often and hoped that in the future I would be able to help others by serving.

My family fled to the banks of a river in eastern Nepal where we ended up living. The sky was our roof, the bare earth was our bed, and the contaminated river water was all we had to sustain us for many days. During that time, we were in desperate need of food, clean water, shelter, and proper clothing. The local Nepali people tried to help us and were able to provide some relief. However, because so many people fled Bhutan and became refugees, conditions rapidly deteriorated. There was no clean drinking water, there was not enough food, and the lack of proper sanitation caused many things to become contaminated. The death toll in the refugee camps rose at an alarming rate; approximately 3-10 people died every day.

As the crisis grew, the United Nations finally focused their attention on our situation. They provided aid to help meet our basic needs. The World Food Program (WFP) provided our food, and United Nations High Commissioner for Refugees (UNHCR) provided clothes and shelter. Throughout Nepal, seven different refugee camps were established. Small huts were built out of bamboo plants, small plastic parts, and any thatch we could find. During the heavy rain and storm, those huts were easily crushed which resulted in all of our belongings becoming soaked and us having to constantly rebuild our temporary homes. Later on, after we had been in the camp for some time, the Association of Medical Doctors in Nepal (AMDA) provided basic health care to the refugees. Also, Caritas Nepal played an important role in educating individuals in the refugee camps. They provided education to refugee children and increased the literacy rate among those of us who were displaced. Life was hard in the camps; there was not much to do to occupy the time.

In Nepal, I became a bachelor student with a science major. Because of this I volunteered my time in the camp as a math and science teacher in the refugee school. When I was young, I was fascinated by all of the help I received from various agencies while I was in the refugee camp. I thought of this often and hoped that in the future I would be able to help others by serving. My family was fortunate. In 2006, the International Organization of Migration (IOM) proposed a third country resettlement as one of the solutions to help get refugees out of the makeshift camps. Seven countries were willing to take in refugees– The United States of America, Canada, Australia, Denmark, New Zealand, United Kingdom, and Norway started resettling refugees. This was so foreign to everyone in the camp, especially myself. I had spent over seventeen years of my life as a refugee on the banks of a river in Nepal without adequate facilities.

Arriving in America

When my family received word that we were being resettled in America, we were ready to search out opportunities and we were looking forward to a new bright future. We ended up in Lansing, Michigan in November 2008. This was a shocking transition- it was like a whole new world. I was in a new environment with new people all around. In the beginning, I felt like I was

> " In the refugee camp, I tried to run after any and all opportunities because they were scarce. In America, opportunities were all around me and they were running after me. When I was a refugee in Nepal, all doors of opportunity were closed, but here in America doors are open everywhere. "

in a dream and had awakened in a new world. In the refugee camp, I tried to run after any and all opportunities because they were scarce. In America, opportunities were all around me and they were running after me. When I was a refugee in Nepal, all doors of opportunity were closed, but here in America doors are open everywhere. I was overwhelmed with opportunity and I wanted to make sure I chose the right door to enter. I had a new hope of a bright future. In the middle of 2009, I started working as assistant case manager at St. Vincent Catholic Charities. This is an organization that helps refugees immigrate and resettle in America. I was given the opportunity to work with many different people and I was familiar with many of the struggles they faced when starting a new life. In the refugee camp, I tried to run after any and all opportunities because they were scarce. In America, opportunities were all around me and they were running after me. When I was a refugee in Nepal, all doors of opportunity were closed, but here in America doors are open everywhere. Bhutan is an agriculturally based society. Being the son of a farmer, gardening is my passion. On one hand I enjoy gardening because it is a lot of fun- on the other hand I like to garden because it is a way to invest your time and energy to help other people in your community. In the refugee camp, we had no land of our own, but we managed to develop good relationships with some local Nepali people, so they gave us a small space to grow food. In Nepal, I learned a lot about gardening, because I watched my parents work. As I got older, I learned even more from them because I helped them on a farm.

I was able to transfer some of this knowledge in Lansing. The Greater Lansing Food Bank (GLB)'s Garden Project provides small gardening plots to the families in the community who are willing to garden to grow and eat their own fresh food. I, along with my family, started gardening at North School garden in 2009. There were many other Bhutanese gardeners at North School with us, as well as at Webster farm, located in the south Lansing. As I began gardening, I quickly learned that the gardening system in the USA differs vastly from the gardening system in Bhutan and Nepal. Many of the other Bhutanese gardeners also had a hard time understanding this because of the language barrier.

As I watched some of my people struggle with gardening here in the

USA, I realized that this was a way I could serve my people. AmeriCorps was a pathway that allowed me to do this. I am grateful and thankful that AmeriCorps came into my life and allowed me this opportunity. As I mentioned earlier, I am a son of a farmer. This was a major reason why I chose to work on the gardening project with AmeriCorps. First, I wanted to use my farming knowledge and experience to help people. Second, I wanted to bridge the communication gap among the Bhutanese people and other gardeners so that they could each share their ideas, strategies, and farming traditions. And finally, I wanted to encourage the Bhutanese people gardening in Lansing to adopt some new techniques for better crop production.

> " We need joint efforts, the old and the new, to make a positive impact on society. Because of the help I received when I was young in the refugee camp, I am always looking for and willing to invest my experiences and knowledge from the past to build into the future. "

As I said before, the gardening system in USA differs vastly from the gardening system of Bhutan or Nepal, due to differences in soil, climatic conditions, and irrigation systems. There is a huge difference between the soil found in Bhutan or Nepal and the soil found in the USA. The soil of Bhutan and Nepal is moist and filled with clay. Watering once a week in that soil is enough to keep the plants green and healthy. However, soil in Lansing is dry and does not hold enough water to keep the soil moist. In Bhutan and Nepal you do not need a hose system for irrigation. People in Bhutan and Nepal actually have to create an irrigation system that drains water from the river and delivers it to the gardens. We did not have hoses in Nepal and Bhutan.

There was plenty of water for irrigation from the river and the soil held water for a long time. In Lansing, I also recommended mulching and pruning unnecessary branches of plants. Mulching helped retain water and it kept the soil moist around the plants. It was easy to mulch using shredded pieces of paper or straw. Pruning unnecessary branches of plants helped enhance the nutrition of the productive parts of the plant to keep it healthy. When I first explained these new techniques to other

Bhutanese people some of them agreed with me. However, others ignored me and told me they had been gardening their whole lives and they knew what to do, they did not need any help. This was hard to deal with because I just wanted to help and I tried to explain that the USA and Nepal and Bhutan were very different places.

Some of the elders had trouble accepting new ways of thinking. They wanted things to remain the same and it was not easy to convince them that there were new and different ways of gardening. When the results from the first round of gardening came in, those who listened and mulched their plants produced better and stronger crops. They had healthier plants. Those who did not embrace the new techniques were shocked that their plants did not produce the same way they did in Bhutan, agreeing that they needed to embrace the new gardening techniques in the future. Finally, after this change of heart, I saw a smile on the faces of my people. I was satisfied because my people appreciated my work and I was able to serve them and help them find new ways of gardening. These new strategies will now be passed on, like they have been for centuries. I learned how to garden and farm from my family, but since we have arrived in America my people and my family have had to add new techniques to the old ways of doing things. We need joint efforts, the old and the new, to make a positive impact on society. Because of the help I received when I was young in the refugee camp, I am always looking for and willing to invest my experiences and knowledge from the past to build into the future. I have learned that life is a journey and there will be good times and bad times and ups and downs. No matter what comes, I have to move forward to pass on my knowledge and to serve other people.

> I am grateful and thankful that AmeriCorps came into my life and allowed me this opportunity.

DILLI R CHAPAGAI became a United States citizen on March 10, 2014. Given this new status he hopes to apply to Peace Corps in the next few months so that he can continue to serve. Currently, Dilli works as an interpreter so that he is able to help other refugees adjust to life in America. If you would like to know more about his story please contact him at dillu_chapagai22@yahoo.com.

Teammates for Life

By Jarrad Plante

Served in NCCC at the Southeast Campus
Charleston, South Carolina

wo college graduates—one from Florida, the other from Massachusetts—gave a year of their lives to serve with AmeriCorps*NCCC. In the fall of 2004, these ambitious "do-gooders" from different parts of the country were brought together and placed on a team (Red Team Three) that truly became a family and were stationed with 300 other corps members on 35 other teams based in Charleston, South Carolina. Over a span of ten months, each person served over 1,800 hours of service with several nonprofits throughout the Southeastern region of the United States, and each of them left the program forever changed.

Our first project lasted six weeks at the Mississippi State Hospital. We engaged nursing home residents with art projects, board games, and field trips to various places, including favorite fishing holes. In addition, we completed much-needed indoor maintenance and outdoor landscape projects for several transitional homes in nearby Jackson. Just before Christmas, the team completed a brief 8-day stint with East Cooper Habitat for Humanity doing construction on several houses. Next, we partnered with the Nature Conservancy in Tennessee for five weeks of trail work in several Nashville parks. During an eight-week educational project at Pinckney Elementary in Mt. Pleasant, South Carolina, we tutored and mentored students, provided whole-class support, supported after-school programming, and completed school improvement projects.

In Covington, Louisiana, our team spent five weeks building houses with Habitat for Humanity. Finally, we spent time with the Fish and Wildlife Service doing invasive species removal and environmental clean-up projects in the Florida Keys.

In addition to learning new skills from these different organizations, this program also taught us to be a part of something bigger than ourselves. We worked on a motivated team of nine others to "Get Things Done for America," and we experienced first-hand the value of being civically engaged and becoming community leaders in whatever communities we found ourselves.

At the same time, we made a lasting impact on the communities we served. Because of our research and recommendations, Pinckney Elementary invested in reusable cafeteria trays and now recycles. We played a part in transforming the culture of an entire school, and the school is now role modeling a more mindful approach to preserving the environment, while saving thousands of dollars a year. The eight different houses we worked on through Habitat for Humanity in Covington were put to the test only three short months after we built them; each one of them withstood the wrath of Hurricane Katrina. And by removing 1.5 acres of metal fencing and illegally dumped trash on Big Pine Key, our team cleared the area around one of the largest watering holes in the Keys, providing much-needed access to fresh water for the local deer. These are only a few examples of the direct impact our service had within the communities we served.

> In addition to learning new skills from these different organizations, this program also taught us to be a part of something bigger than ourselves.

Joining AmeriCorps*NCCC was truly just the beginning for the two of us. We were so inspired by our AmeriCorps experience that we became teammates for life! Jordan and I got married on 7/11/09. Most of our team, along with family and friends, were present at the ceremony and were a part of our wedding weekend on Long Boat Key. The two of us continue to dedicate our lives to service.

After working for several years with the Boy Scouts of America, I resigned my position as District Executive to utilize my AmeriCorps education award and complete my master's degree in public policy. Additionally, thanks to a great partnership between the Nonprofit Leadership Alliance (formally American Humanics) and *NCCC, I was fortunate to have used the rest of my Eli Segal education award to earn my certificate in Nonprofit Management and Leadership and become a CNP – Certified Nonprofit Professional. For both programs, I was allowed to utilize my *NCCC experience as part of my internship.

> " It's a program worth having; it's a program worth continuing to grow and expand to allow many other inspiring young leaders the opportunity to serve America while developing into active citizens. "

Jordan has continued working with AmeriCorps programs since she graduated from *NCCC. She and another NCCC teammate were corps members for the National Preparedness Response Corps through the American Red Cross in Seattle, Washington. I recall flying across the country to visit her in early September 2005, just after Hurricane Katrina hit the gulf coast. In lieu of a full vacation, the two of us spent the first half of my trip working together on a crisis hotline, answering phone calls at the office from desperate people reaching out to the Red Cross from cell phones as they were sitting on their rooftops in New Orleans, just trying to survive the storm. After a couple of very full days, we were able to help folks who were searching for loved ones register in a database so they could be found by their families.

Since I had a job working for the Boy Scouts back home in Massachusetts during Jordan's second stint as an AmeriCorps member, she decided to move up to the Bay State. She found an opportunity working for City Year Rhode Island, another AmeriCorps-funded organization that engages young adults to serve full-time and help struggling students stay in school and on track to graduate. She worked her way up from Admissions Manager to Recruitment Director to Deputy Director and was even interim Executive Director while her boss was on maternity leave, all in five short years.

Then, as timing would have it, just after I graduated from grad school, there was an opportunity to open a new City Year site in Orlando. Our relationship was built on supporting each other. Jordan had moved up to New England for me and had been on board with me quitting my job and attending school, so, it was only fitting that I return the favor and continue our adventure together in the "AmeriWorld" with a new challenge.

As we were making plans for Orlando, Jordan was asked to take a three-month detour to Miami and lead a young group of staff members in the development department. After our mini stopover in Miami, we began our quest helping to start up City Year Orlando (CYO). Jordan was hired as the start-up director and she in turn hired a skeleton team to begin recruiting corps members, fundraising, building a board of directors, and cultivating relationships in the community. I helped in all of these areas as City Year Orlando's Operation's Consultant.

As CYO was ready to move into its founding year, Jordan was hired as their Executive Director, a position she never thought she would hold. At the same time, I enrolled into a doctoral program – Educational Leadership & Policy Studies for Higher Education, at the University of Central Florida (UCF) and was able to transfer two courses from my CNP certificate program as my cognate classes in my EdD plan of study – maximizing my education award toward three different educational programs. I also became the Community Service Graduate Assistant for Volunteer UCF, whose mission is to provide civic engagement opportunities to the UCF student body. Currently, I advise student leaders who become expert educators by planning and implementing service events based on their social topic: Health, Domestic Abuse, and Hunger and Homelessness, to name a few. Additionally, I applied as a regional representative in AmeriCorps*NCCC's newest initiative – Alumni Leadership Council, meeting other alums, promoting the program, co-hosting a team, and even joining City Year Orlando and a team in the southeast region for a day of physical service.

The last team activity that Jordan and I worked on together was sitting on a planning committee for *The State of the Research on Civic Engagement: How Service and Volunteerism is Reshaping our Civic and*

Community Health, co-chaired by the director for the Center for Public and Nonprofit Management and the Corporation for National and Community Service regional office in Orlando with Wendy Spenser, CEO of CNCS, as our key note speaker.

It is hard to believe that Jordan and I were randomly put on a team with other 18-24 year-olds ten years ago, to better the communities in the southeastern United States. The transformation, however, was how AmeriCorps*NCCC has served us. The two of us reflect on how blessed we are to have been on such an amazing team and ending up together. Service to others is a lifestyle for Jordan and I, one that we want to continue, while encouraging other young leaders to serve as well.

> " I hope others who read these excerpts will become inspired to celebrate, serve, and support AmeriCorps. "

AmeriCorps has changed our lives and it has changed the lives and circumstances of so many in this country. It's a program worth having; it's a program worth continuing to grow and expand to allow many other inspiring young leaders the opportunity to serve America while developing into active citizens.

I consider myself the luckiest guy being married to someone so incredibly selfless, compassionate, and inspiring and who also has enough room in her heart to love me, support me in continuing my education, and be my best friend. The two of us are celebrating our five-year anniversary this July and we just booked a beach house on Folly Beach in Charleston, South Carolina where our AmeriCorps team will get together Labor Day Weekend for our 10-year reunion. I hope others who read these excerpts will become inspired to celebrate, serve, and support AmeriCorps.

JARRAD PLANTE is working on a doctorate in Educational Leadership & Policy Studies for Higher Education at the University of Central Florida and a Graduate Assistant for Volunteer UCF. Jordan Plante currently works as the Executive Director for City Year Orlando. Together, J&J continue to "get things done for America" by serving their local community. Contact Info: jarrad. plante@gmail.com

Umuntu ngumuntu ngamantu

By **Cristina Bacor**

Served with City Year
Boston, Massachusetts

I t's called AmeriCorps," Emily said as she reached her left arm over her head, reaching behind her, face up toward the sun in her exaulted warrior pose. Emily with her dreadlocks and lavender smell. Emily who loved feeling the sun on her face and walking barefoot in the grass. Emily from Vermont. Me from Texas.

I learned much more than how to speak Spanish that semester abroad in Granada. I met Emily. The kindest, most positive, most liberal person I had ever met. Nearing the end of our semester abroad, we had several conversations about what we would do when we returned stateside. Of all the people I studied abroad with, she was my favorite. We volunteered in town together. She taught yoga in Spanish and I taught English.

"Are you sure you want to do AmeriCorps?" she asked me. "You've been talking about decorating an apartment in Houston and getting a job."

I had been talking about decorating an apartment, incessantly. I was home sick after five months away. And I saw some candle holders I desperately wanted for a hall table I did not yet own.

"I don't know," I told her while trying to exalt my warrior. I was still unsure if AmeriCorps was the right decision. Decisions 5,385 miles from home seemed harder, and this was my first time doing yoga. This was also hard.

I spent some time on the internet researching different AmeriCorps programs and had become most comfortable with a program called City Year. On the City Year application, it asks where you would like to be placed.

> We wore Timberlands and red jackets and kids knew us and trusted us around the city.

"Where do I want to be placed?" I thought to myself. Where do I want to be? What are my choices? Philadelphia, New York, Chicago. I didn't want to go back to Texas so soon after I had discovered my liberal self and yoga. I submitted to City Year I was willing to go where they needed me and hoped it wasn't San Antonio.

My interview was that week. I was excited to be able to say, "I'm sorry if there is a delay, I'm calling from Spain." This was my first trip out of the country and my second trip out of Texas. A college girlfriend and I went to New York the March before my trip to Spain. I wasn't about to go out of country without having seen New York first.

I studied public relations in college and fully expected to start a career at an agency, but somehow that didn't feel right and I had trouble getting interviews overseas. I decided to focus on my community and not myself, and that is when Emily told me about AmeriCorps. "Core" as in core of your being, not corpse, as in a dead person.

~

"What are you doing?" my friend Cerise said to me puzzled, "What is that?" I was staying with Cerise in Houston until I needed to move to Boston, where City Year wanted me to be.

If my mom gave me any grief about my decision to move so far north, I don't remember or I blocked it out. I was excited about City Year. It was unlike anything my friends in Texas were doing.

I traveled further south to my family's home in Mission, Texas to pack up my things. And by pack, I mean I threw all my clothes, favorite books and music into the trunk of my car. My dad "unpacked" my trunk and repacked my things in boxes and bags. My parents wanted to drive me to Boston. We drove for two days and I remember Pennsylvania. Somewhere on the way up we saw a man driving a car with a University of Houston sticker.

"Go Coogs!" I yelled to him from the backseat window. He smiled, surprised and threw up his Cougar paw, our alma mater hand sign. We stopped in Pennsylvania for a night and when we got to Boston the next day we unpacked all my things on the floor. I had no furniture. My new roommate offered me an extra mattress she brought from her home in Connecticut and I said goodbye to my parents. They stayed long enough to unpack my things, but the drive back to Texas was long and they needed to get back on the road. Somehow, this goodbye was worse than the goodbye before Spain.

My new roommate, Heidi, and I walked down Centre Street in Jamaica Plain, where we now lived. We stopped in at a resale shop and I eyed a twin bed frame. There was already a desk in my room and I had one of those plastic drawer sets from Target. I wouldn't need much else right away. After strolling through the resale shop, we stopped at the Purple Cactus for a burrito and I ran across the street to get a job application from JP Licks,

> " My AmeriCorps experience started with Emily. Emily, an AmeriCorps alumna, who taught me that people need each other. And, it is our responsibility to care for one another. "

a neighborhood ice cream shop. I had about a month until my "year of service" started and I wanted to make a little extra money before I was not able to because of my commitment to City Year.

I started working at JP Licks the next week and served Joey McIntyre, from New Kids on the Block, an ice cream cone. He has sparkly eyes. Jordan Knight had always been my favorite New Kid. It was always his lines I would sing in front of the bathroom mirror. I wish I remembered what kind of ice cream Joey ordered because it was the highlight of my summer.

~

By the time our first day at City Year came around, I had two more roommates. Another from Connecticut and one from Tennessee. "Good, another southerner," I thought.

Felicia (Connecticut) taught me how to ride on public transportation. We got on the T at Forest Hills and got off at Back Bay. The speed at which the train doors opened and closed gave me anxiety. Back Bay Station was bustling and there was a Dunkin' Donuts on every corner. Where I'm from, people are in buildings and they use cars to get to work. This environment of people, trains and cars also gave me anxiety. The intersection of all three seemed chaotic, but overtime it became natural to me and I preferred it to driving cars. Driving cars in Boston isn't easy, anyhow. The streets don't make any sense and they are very narrow. My daddy's truck would do no good in Boston.

Felicia, Heidi, Mary (Tennessee) and I sat near the front of the room for our orientation. Other groups of roommates sat together excitedly talking and everyone scoping everyone else out. It was like college orientation, but much, much smaller. That day we learned about City Year. We learned how we should come dressed to serve, we learned something called a "readiness check," we learned that shaking your hands, fingertips toward the sky, was silent applause and that it helped moved the day a long. We learned that if someone has their hand up you stop talking until everyone else stops talking. We learned that the next week we would be going to camp and we would be assigned our teams.

Umuntu ngumuntu ngamantu

Some of us would work in schools, others of us would work in the office preparing for physical service days or preparing for weekend middle school and high school programs. All of us would tutor.

I tutored at the Mattahunt Learning Center in Mattapan. Mattapan was also referred to as "Murder-pan". My team and I taught social justice and service learning to our students in the after school program. One of my students was the son of a police administrator who had sold out the mob, or so I was told by a learning center staff person. We wore

Timberlands and red jackets and kids knew us and trusted us around the city.

We organized a Martin Luther King Day March for Peace in Boston's Roxbury neighborhood in January. We found hypodermic needles in the mulch of children's playgrounds. We hosted spring break camps where I taught inner-city pre-teens how to meditate.

> "I am a person through other people. My humanity is tied to yours."

~

My AmeriCorps experience started with Emily. Emily, an AmeriCorps alumna, who taught me that people need each other. And, it is our responsibility to care for one another. Emily who taught me yoga and meditation. Emily who taught me what Umuntu ngumuntu ngamantu meant before City Year:

"I am a person through other people. My humanity is tied to yours."

It was this learning that put me on my true path. I was never meant to work at a PR agency; I was meant to help people. My experience at City Year, and with AmeriCorps has led me to non-profit fundraising where I help organizations live Ubuntu.

Emily lives in Oregon, in a barn, with her chickens. Emily, you should see my exalted warrior now.

CRISTINA BACOR is committed to education, social justice, and equality for all. She relishes work with organizations to create opportunities for people to build better lives for themselves. Cristina is a Senior Director with CCS and is currently in Indianapolis with the Kiwanis International Foundation and the global campaign to eliminate maternal and neonatal tetanus, The Eliminate Project. This UNICEF partnership will raise $110 million to save or protect more than 61 million mothers and babies from tetanus.

Service and the Search for Self

By Kyle Kent

* Names have been changed

Served in an AmeriCorps National
Program with Habitat for Humanity
Bend, Oregon

oining AmeriCorps and embarking on a year of National Service, for me, was initially an unclear and uninformed decision. However, it was one of the best I've ever made. Originally, my only exposure to AmeriCorps, prior to my own enrollment, came from a distant university friend. She would return to campus after holidays full of enticing information about social injustice and generational poverty on Navajo Reservations in Arizona. She was a carpentry apprentice. It all sounded confusing, but at the same time awesome. Regrettably, I never looked enough into the AmeriCorps program she was a part of because it seemed too distant.

I grew more aware of the looming reality of a fast approaching graduation, and the subsequent terrors of job hunting. As a liberal arts graduate with a Bachelor's degree, I knew job hunting would be a daunting task. I became increasingly open to any and all future possibilities. Immediately after graduating, I left Ohio in a fury of manifest destiny idealism. I moved my few possessions via a rickety four door sedan to rural northern California to work as a farm hand on a

. . . .
51

massive and ultra secluded cattle ranch. My cowboy fantasy day job was short lived once I realized how distant my rudimentary and laborious daily workload was from the justifications that surrounded having a Bachelor's degree. Thus I left my transitory home on the range in search for a more inspirational and purposeful place amongst the work force. About this time, I came under another slightly disillusioned impression that I should learn how to build a house. I would drive from internet connection to internet connection emailing various construction companies and carpenters around the Northwest to see if they'd like to host an intern or bestow an apprenticeship. Understandably, they all said no. Graciously, however, one of the companies recommended that without experience I should start volunteering with Habitat for Humanity.

It was a good idea but the impending dark clouds of college debt were beginning to accumulate and I needed a monetary solution. The first Habitat for Humanity affiliate I emailed was Bend Oregon, and to this date, that has been the most prolific email of my life. Their straightforward response to my predicament was simple: "Join AmeriCorps Nationals, move to Bend, and we'll employ you for the duration of your service year as a Site Supervisor." Eagerly I read the literature, acknowledged the halved wages, drooled over the prospects of the Segal Education Award, and almost at once packed everything I owned into my Buick. I steered towards an unfamiliar community, to work an unfamiliar job and satisfy a year of National Service with the Bend Area Habitat for Humanity.

The isolationism of working as a ranch hand in the mountainous back country of California couldn't have prepared me for the rapid immersion I experienced with Habitat's team and the greater community of Bend Oregon. Working with cows and horses everyday was a far cry from the volunteer groups, churches, and local schools I was almost instantaneously charged with supervising and educating about the necessity for local-low income housing solutions. It was a welcome shift. I was the only AmeriCorps member serving in Bend with Habitat for Humanity. I quickly became a useful asset to the organization due to my willingness to learn and take on less desirable jobs such as attic insulation or under-floor dryer ventilation pipe laying. As soon as I got my bearings, I was drafted onto the Neighborhood Revitalization Initiative team and began making regular home visits to perform project assessments for new applicants throughout the city.

When you are a student at a large state university in Ohio, you are typically surrounded by like-minded, similarly aged, middle class students from Cincinnati, Columbus, or Cleveland on any given day. For my four years as a student this was my peer group. Unfortunately that perpetuated a sort of demographically isolated view of the community and my role. It caused me to forget and become ignorant to the diversity beyond the campus walls. Working as a Site Supervisor through the Neighborhood Revitalization Initiative was my re-initiation into the broader diversity of local communities and I became fascinated by the connections I was having the opportunity to make with the people I served.

> **The first Habitat for Humanity affiliate I emailed was Bend Oregon, and to this date, that has been the most prolific email of my life.**

The team I was a part of would work five days a week for months, in and around the homes of families throughout the city. Our tasks included installing hand rails or wheel chair ramps for disabled and aging veterans, insulating the attics and under-floors of family homes to promote energy efficiency thus reducing utility costs. We led neighborhood clean-ups, built community fences, and painted or repaired the exteriors of deteriorating homes. These tasks became opportunities to reintroduce myself as a member of the community. This work opened my eyes to individuals, needs, and families that previously escaped my attention.

The amount of housing assistance needed in the community became a huge motivator during my service year. Getting to know the individual families and knowing their struggles and concerns, provided a mental strength to work long hours in winter snow while enduring splinters and aching muscles. AmeriCorps and the idea of National Service, which were once an unknown and distant possibility, became a point of pride. Seeing the results of our efforts, and how quickly we affected change, altered my reasons for working with a National Service program. In the beginning, I was selfishly looking for a way to expand on a whim of an interest: how to build a house. But as the year went on, I transitioned from working for myself to working for others. The more volunteers I worked with and the more families in the community I served, the less and less I thought about my resume and personal vocational quests. Helping others was my new focus. The mindset became, "Yes I can help you and I can start right now." I was glad to have become that person. Explaining what AmeriCorps actually is and how a year of service really worked developed into a regular feature of my job. I speculated that other people in alternative service programs around the country were struggling with that same task. As my year with Bend Area Habitat for Humanity progressed, I began to fully comprehend the worth of my work and the work of AmeriCorps in general.

The city of Bend experienced a substantial population boom from about 2002-2008, causing the once sleepy mountain community to swell about the size of New England. Due to this, there was a large industry for new home construction and many new companies flocked to Bend during those years. When the housing bubble popped, and the realities of the economic crisis settled in, Bend was left with a large unsupported housing construction industry. Homes became excessively costly, and new construction for affordable housing halted abruptly. Yet the demand for low income and cost effective housing remains.

> In the beginning, I was selfishly looking for a way to expand on a whim of an interest: how to build a house. But as the year went on, I transitioned from working for myself to working for others.

Bend Area Habitat for Humanity became one of the few remaining organizations in Central Oregon to assist with affordable housing and home repair solutions. By spring of that year, we were beginning to build our fourth home. By summer we had fully housed fifteen low-income family members, most of whom were single mothers. I had participated in and completed twenty-one Neighborhood Revitalization Initiative critical home repairs and weatherization projects throughout the city. Many of these projects maximized mobility for aging citizens, fixed leaking roofs, and decreased energy bills by thousands of dollars.

I had the privilege of co-leading a complete home remodel project. The elderly couple who received the home had Dementia. By expanding door ways, insulating the newly installed wood floors, building accessibility ramps, and redesigning a bathroom for wheelchair mobility they were able to live comfortably. The Habitat affiliate I was serving through became one of the most successful and productive in the country for home repair and energy efficiency promotion programs. I am proud to have helped them meet needs everyday. Through this experience as an AmeriCorps National member, I was able to connect with new faces in the community which were previously unknown to me. One family, whose accessibility ramps I built, still call whenever they are having a party or family get together so that I can "Come over and meet everyone!" One patron was a Native American D-Day surviving veteran. As I fixed his attic, he would sneak me into his radio laboratory and teach me the methodology behind HAM radio ethics. These friendships constantly rejuvenated my year of service and dramatically expanded my sense of community and home.

Another parallel AmeriCorps team is called the Clean Energy Service Corps. They are a local, six-month crew of seven young service members. Many of these students decided not to pursue further education or their High School diplomas. I supervised these young adults almost everyday. They helped complete construction projects and various assignments throughout the city. If they completed a certain amount of designated hours with me and Habitat For Humanity, they were offered an opportunity to earn their GED, Duct Sealing Licenses, and provided an educational award to be used for tuition at an in-state university or college. Two crews I oversaw were initially resistant to direction, not wanting to do less desirable jobs. However, both crews experienced significant growth as a team and as individuals during their time in the programs. Not only did they grow excited about being offered the opportunity to learn green construction practices and non-profit solutions, they grew more excited about their own future. A majority of the Clean Energy Service Corps members used their educational awards to pursue GED's, Associates, and Bachelors degrees. I can proudly say that most of them are currently employed. Supervising younger and shorter-lived AmeriCorps crews was at times highly challenging and stressful. However, in the long run, it was gratifying to assist a program that was a vessel for positively impacting the community.

> " My indirect and seemingly happenstance path towards joining a yearlong service program turned into a reeducation in the foundations of selflessness and community partnerships. "

Right about that time, I decided to continue working with Bend Area Habitat For Humanity for a second year as an AmeriCorps National construction site supervisor. The Executive Director offered me a full time position as a Site Coordinator. The offer took me by surprise. I had become immersed and integrated into the organization and so invested in the projects so the answer was simply yes. I accepted the offer to work full time in new construction and the Neighborhood Revitalization Initiative. The opportunity to continue serving families of Bend, and promote positive change in low income housing markets turned out to be exactly what I wanted. Before AmeriCorps, I felt as if I were floating from concept to concept. I was chasing ideas about personal productivity and growth without ever accomplishing anything. My indirect and seemingly happenstance path towards joining a yearlong service program turned into a reeducation in the foundations of selflessness and community partnerships. My impulse desire to learn how to build homes was satisfied along with learning how to build relationships.

Currently, my full time position with Bend Area Habitat For Humanity is mirroring my former service year; it's a continuum. Positive changes within the community of Bend were initiated through direct service by AmeriCorps members. As an AmeriCorps member, I grew from relationships with volunteers, businesses, and families. All of the lessons I learned during last year continue to provide me with a strong foundation.

My supervisor always tells me, "Never throw away your tools. As long as you have them you'll have work. You have no excuse not to help someone." The ways in which I continue to impact communities is growing. Additionally, the more time I spend with Bend Area Habitat, the more I am able to apply what I've learned in new ways. The training I've received in volunteer management and green building practices is being utilized exponentially. The area offices have recently expanded operations to a smaller city, east of Bend, called Prineville. The Neighborhood Revitalization team I am a part of has renewed its long-range efforts in exterior and critical home repairs in the greater Prineville area. This has been a much-awaited effort by the community and is showing extremely positive results. In the last six months we have successfully weatherized and insulated six houses and moved two families into remodeled and revitalized homes. They are first time property owners.

The expansion of our outreach has continued in more dramatic ways as well. I am writing from a beautiful hostel courtyard in Antigua, Guatemala. I just recently left another team of twelve Bend area Habitat For Humanity volunteers in Santa Rosa de Copan, Honduras. An extension of Habitat for Humanity is called Global Village program. They provide local community volunteers an opportunity to partner with Habitat and one other international affiliate in Central America. Our mission was to help local Honduran staff dedicate 20 two bedroom brick and mortar homes in the El Rosario neighborhood of Santa Rosa. We also assisted in the completion of a community center and playground for the new low-income housing neighborhood. Not only did this mission provide the Honduran Habitat staff and soon to be homeowners with assistance and labor necessary to meet construction deadlines, it also provided an opportunity for international volunteers from Bend Oregon to experience the scale and scope of Habitat For Humanity's global mission.

> " I am deeply grateful for the opportunity of discovering the many hidden layers in each community. I am equally thankful for the lasting relationship built through day-to-day service. "

The trip was an exceptional and educational experience; I expect the volunteers will return to Bend eager to become more involved on the domestic and local level. Personally, this Global Village trip served as confirmation for fresh direction I am eager to implement in Bend. AmeriCorps has ingrained a culture of service into my perspective of community.

As my year of service came to a close I constantly thought about the thousands of people around the country who were completing their own year. It was comforting to recall the immense amounts of productivity that came from such selflessness. I am deeply grateful for the opportunity of discovering the many hidden layers in each community. I am equally thankful for the lasting relationship built through day-to-day service.

KYLE KENT continues to work full time as the Site Coordinator for Bend Area Habitat for Humanity. Providing critical support to both new construction crews and the Neighborhood Revitalization Initiative and it's affiliated programs throughout Oregon.

Heart Hot, Head Cold

· ·

By **Samantha Mairson**

Served in NCCC at the Southwest Campus
Denver, Colorado

S amantha Mairson," I said. I removed my ID from my wallet and placed it on the booth counter between us. My ID was received by a middle-aged woman wearing an AmeriCorps NCCC shirt and a smile. She marked my name on a list, gave me further instructions, and handed me items indicating my progression with the in-processing process. I remember the red plastic strip of tagging. "It indicates the team you are on," she informed me, instructing me to tie it on my luggage.

I arrived at Denver International Airport on October 9, 2012. I was sick, my hair was cut short, I wasn't wearing makeup, and I still hadn't shaved my legs.

I was ready to make friends.

This was the first day of my 10 month service commitment with the NCCC's Southwest Region campus. From late April through late September of that year, I had been part of the California Conservation Corps' Backcountry Trails Program. It was an AmeriCorps-affiliated state and national program that changed my life. The Backcountry Program enabled me to *live* conservation, build trails, and learn more about my capabilities than I had developed in the 18 years prior. When my CCC graduation ceremony in Yosemite National Park ended, my family gently shuffled me away from the mountains that had become my second

· · · · · · ·

home. It was late September. The days were becoming shorter and colder. AmeriCorps NCCC was my next commitment.

I followed the baggage claim signs and found myself in the bustling heart of the airport, surrounded by people chasing similar and dissimilar destinations. Having checked in with AmeriCorps personnel, I followed the crowds to baggage claim. Then I followed instructions to wait by the exit doors for a bus that would shuttle my new comrades and I to Loretta Heights University, home of the NCCC Southwest Region Campus.

> We learned what it meant to be a wildland firefighter and more than that – we learned what it meant to be a team.

AmeriCorps taught me that community service always looks different.

We zoomed down a long stretch of highway, racing towards mountains and communities that most of us had not yet met. When I say community service always looks different, I mean to say it looks like a brigade of coach buses full of people from across the country, ages 18-24, descending on a small campus (once used as a Catholic girls' high school) in Denver, Colorado. The people are varied shades of white chocolate, milk chocolate, and dark chocolate. People speak like Chicago, like Boston, like California, like Connecticut. People move like book smart, like street smart, sometimes both and sometimes neither. Some watch, some sleep, some write in journals or snap "selfies" on their smart phones.

Community service with AmeriCorps first appears like a series of regular interactions between regular people. Meal time talk falls back on TV shows and life stories. The invisible decision maker drops pieces on the game board and friendships are born out of seemingly chance circumstances.

"What do you need?"

"Hey, how are you?"

"Samantha. And you?"

"Where are you from?"

"How can I help?"

"How do I do this?"

"Thank you!"

"You're welcome."

"What are you doing later?"

I was placed on a game board of 8 states in the southwestern region of the United States and my commitment to service resulted in my serving (primarily) the communities of:

Denver, CO
Farmington, NM,
Colorado Springs, CO,
Daisy, AK,
and Bluff City, AK.

Denver, Colorado was base camp. Our first month of training took place in Denver. As a part of training, we took part in a series of small, day-long service projects in the surrounding community. We learned about disaster response and about the AmeriCorps program. We trained for job roles on our teams and we took part in what was essentially a month-long interview process, both with our teammates and our bosses. I learned about the Denver transportation system and about the local dive bar that served as the setting for AmeriCorps stuff of legends. I learned why people had come to AmeriCorps and what expectations they had of themselves and of the program. I learned that Denver was a huge community to serve and that the need for service was great. A highlight of my Denver-based training time included a day of service at the Denver Green School. I was with my newly formed fire management team and we spent the day volunteering in the school garden, the cafeteria, the library, the student-run organic garden, and a variety of classes.

> My conviction is that community service enables you to be completely human, imperfect and impactful.

I plan to return to the Denver Green School.

My first project round was picked. My team and I would be spending 6 weeks of our service calendar in the community of Farmington, New Mexico. I had the job role of "service learning initiator". It was my responsibility to have the team reflect on service and learn about the community we were serving. My team lived and worked in the Farmington Boys & Girls Club. For this project, we were able to very directly engage with the people in the community. Farmington borders a Navajo reservation, so we served a very diverse and primarily low-income community. Every day, at about 3pm, a mob of kids, grades K-12, would descend on the club. It was our job to keep them entertained and to look after them. One of my favorite parts about this project was our proximity to the local library. I was able to do an incredible amount of independent service project work at the nearby public library. The library gave me a great way to connect with the community and gain experience in a line of work that I would like to pursue as a part of my personal long-term goals. I was invited and encouraged by the head children's librarian to return as an AmeriCorps VISTA worker and serve in her library again, in a longer-term capacity.

My next project in Colorado Springs, Colorado was assigned to my team by virtue of our being a fire management team. We were partnered with the El Paso Sheriff's Department and trained as a hand crew resource for combatting wildland fire. We were housed in an active detention center, which greatly impacted the general crew mood. Additionally, it was winter and we spent the better part of everyday chainsawing in the snow-covered, overgrown Black Forest groves of ponderosa pine. The work was challenging; the impact measurable; the days long, cold, and monotonous. We were ill-equipped with glove protection against the cold, as our fire gloves were leather and acted better as refrigerators than ovens. For the second part of service we were housed in central downtown Colorado Springs. That round, we mitigated 1.5 square acres of the Black Forest, becoming chainsaw certified (a skill that many of us would later appreciate).

> "That was the most extraordinary part of AmeriCorps: it expected me to be a part of something bigger than *myself, my* goals, *my* plans. They were *our* goals, *our* plans."

That spring, some 15,000 acres of the Pike's Peak region Black Forest would burn, taking 2 lives and 500+ houses with it. It would take the title of most devastating fire in Colorado history and we would be first responders on that fire. We would later learn that the area we mitigated was unaffected when the fire reached it.

Everything around it burned.

For my fourth and final round, I returned with my original team to Colorado Springs. The opportunity to serve the community directly re-emerged when the fires kicked up in June. Colorado Springs was busy commemorating the anniversary of the devastating Waldo Canyon Fire, when the Black Forest Fire began. My team had just been on our first "spike-out", overnight fire response at the Air Force Academy when we got the call.

> It is nice to feel like part of a team, part of community, part of an effort to make the world maybe just a little bit better than it was when you woke up the day before.

We arrived on scene and the distant forest greeted us with a plume of smoke the likes of which I had never seen. It was the foreshadowing to a "spike" that would last longer than a week, with long and arduous work days running into each other. We followed orders, we tried not to get ourselves killed, we learned what it meant to be a wildland firefighter and more than that – we learned what it meant to be a team. At the end of our day shifts, we rolled back into fire basecamp and were greeted and cheered by crowds swinging signs. It was the kind of "thank you" we hadn't yet experienced on the job. We walked, sometimes to the tune of blisters, in three parades. I think those are the glory moments that people imagine when they imagine serving a community to the fullest extent possible.

In serving these communities, I learned about them. That was the immediate trade-off and I knew it from the beginning. I gave my time to a cause I believed to be worthy but during that time, I also learned, made friendships, and improved skills. My conviction is that community service enables you to be completely human, imperfect and impactful.

The best community servers are not there by fluke or chance. They serve a community with direction, with purpose, with intention, and the best of the best serve with passion. In the future I will take the many lessons of my AmeriCorps experience and serve the communities in which I belong.

~

Sometimes I wish I was part of a culture that asked me to help. No one ever really asks me to help or expects me to chip in, to sweat. No one automatically expects me to be a teammate,

> to lend a hug,
> to lend a shoulder,
> to lend an ear,
> to lend a hand.

That was the most extraordinary part of AmeriCorps: it expected me to be a part of something bigger than *myself, my* goals, *my* plans. They were *our* goals, *our* plans.

> " The same goes for community service. You can come back to it anytime you like, and with my memories of it, I know – in my heart and in my head – I always will. "

"Somehow I don't think their insurance would cover that," the man on my right says in response to my expressed desire to help the airplane people load our baggage. We have been delayed by a great, big blizzard and are being de-iced on the Chicago Midway runway. I have spent many hours sitting, waiting. I am on a flight though now, again bound for Denver International Airport. I am visiting old friends, old bosses; a year has passed. In coming days, this year's fresh crop of corps members will be making their way back to campus from holiday break.

Sitting and waiting were options in AmeriCorps, but they were not the best, most reasonable or most automatic ones. Not for me, at least.

Freedom, autonomy, and independence are beautiful gifts, but left alone they can transform into just that: being alone. It is nice to feel like part of a team, part of community, part of an effort to make the world maybe just a little bit better than it was when you woke up the day before. I may not always be able to serve with my Class 19A AmeriCorps teammates, but I will always serve with them in my heart and in my head.

During a time of hardship, a wise, fellow corps member told me, "Keep your heart hot, head cold. Heart hot, head cold."

When you apply that formula to a life of community service, or any life really, you will establish a habit of acting decisively, analytically, critically, and with compassion. I believe it is with a lukewarm head and a hot heart that I served the communities of America during my months of service. As I continue to indulge my passion for community service, I will always strive to improve that balance.

Heart hot, head cold.

And a boot on the ground.

My plane lands in Denver and this time I'm alone. The feeling of being alone doesn't last long.

When I left the CCC Backcountry Trails Program, the program director said to us, "The mountains will always be here. You can come back to them any time you like." The same goes for community service. You can come back to it anytime you like, and with my memories of it, I know – in my heart and in my head – I always will.

I picked up my bags from the luggage carousel and shortly thereafter, began stretching my tired limbs. I was doing yoga in the baggage claim area, when a young, air force serviceman approached me. He made a joke and within minutes we were talking like old friends.

"Samantha Mairson," I said, smiling, and I shook his hand.

SAMANTHA MAIRSON is currently hiking the Appalachian Trail! She is returning to the University of Connecticut in the fall to finish her bachelor's degree. She is an aspiring librarian.

Still Standing

. . . .

By Dwight R. Owens

Served in an AmeriCorps State and National
Program with Project LINC AmeriCorps
LIFE (Living Independence for Everyone) of Mississippi
Mississippi Statewide

AmeriCorps gave me a new purpose. For me, it was life-changing. As a miracle survivor, it helped lead me from tragedy to triumph.

Prior to the year of 2005, I, Dwight Owens, was a 23-year old math teacher and football coach. I was content in my life and career. My way of life screeched to a halt when I was hit by a drunk driver in August, 2005 on my way to school. My survival of the accident is considered a miracle. Rear-ended by a 71 year-old drunk driver, my injuries included punctured lungs, six broken ribs, severe internal injuries, a broken back, a dislodged liver and a severed spine. I also coded in the emergency room and was given up for dead. I stayed in the hospital for nearly a year, first on life support, then Intensive Care, and then finally began my road to recovery. Permanently paralyzed from the waist down, I spent two years in a constant cycle of rehabilitation, surgery and medical set-backs, but an indomitable will and deep faith kept me focused. Against all odds, I survived.

I dedicated the life I nearly lost to serving others. Keeping a promise I made to God, I began sharing my story to inspire others, advancing the cause of the disabled, and speaking against drugs and alcohol. I was later introduced to AmeriCorps, which helped maximize my purpose.

. . . .

From 2009 through 2011, I served as an AmeriCorps Project LINC (Linking Individuals Into Neighborhoods and Communities) member with L.I.F.E (Living Independence For Everyone) of Mississippi. L.I.F.E's exclusive mission is to give people with disabilities the confidence and skills to be independent. Person-by-person, day-by-day, they offer people a new sense of hope, pride, and self-reliance. This not only brings great happiness to the person learning these skills, it also helps families and the broader community. In fact, many, probably even most, of the employees at L.I.F.E are alumnae of their program, and when they go to work at L.I.F.E, they are proud with no excuses. Every person, no matter the disability, is expected to meet the highest standards of the profession. To my way of thinking, that's a pretty good program.

> AmeriCorps is a great program for people with disabilities. It connects them to the different resources available, makes them feel good about themselves, and builds character.

As an AmeriCorps member in the Project LINC program, I provided peer support to over 1,200 individuals with disabilities. I completed 48 ADA (Americans With Disabilities Act) site surveys to ensure accessibility for persons with disabilities, and provided over 300 life skills training sessions to increase independence for Mississippians with disabilities. I also helped many individuals transition from public institutions to their own homes and started a "Men with Disabilities" support group, encouraging independence and leadership. As a result of my AmeriCorps service, many Mississippians with disabilities are active, productive members of their communities. My efforts have not gone unnoticed. I received the AmeriCorps National Spirit of Service Award in 2010 for being an outstanding AmeriCorps member. The award was received at the Corporation for National and Community Service's 2010 National Conference on Volunteering and Service.

AmeriCorps is a great program for people with disabilities. It connects them to the different resources available, makes them feel good about themselves, and builds character. Just because someone has a disability doesn't mean they can't contribute. People with disabilities serve for the same reasons as anyone else: to give back to their communities, and to become more active and engaged. Many find that service offers real-life work experience, allowing opportunities to test career paths, sharpen skills, and define employment goals and interests.

After AmeriCorps, I continued my individual journey in service. Being paralyzed and living life in a wheelchair, I take great joy in advocating for people with disabilities. I realize that for anyone disability may only be an accident away; I personally know *that* better than anyone. Therefore, I like to help people realize that when they advocate for people with disabilities, they may be advocating for themselves one day as well.

Turning my tragedy into a positive, I also enjoy making motivational "Before You Drink, Think Dwight" presentations whenever I can, to caution people of all ages against drugs and alcohol. I am not in the business of scaring people. Using my testimony and motivation tactics, I show

> " I speak forgiveness as a better path than hatred or vengeance. "

them that bad things happen to innocent people when you drink and drive. I am also in the business of teaching responsibility to youngsters and showing them what they can accomplish no matter the odds. I fill my talks with humor, funny anecdotes, and serious tales of people with disabilities. Each talk is sprinkled with laughter and tears. I explain that I forgave the driver that put me in a wheelchair, and I speak forgiveness as a better path than hatred or vengeance.

AmeriCorps service helped shape me into who I am today. Volunteering and service mean a lot to me. It means knowing I can make a difference. It means engaging with my community and extending myself beyond my direct, personal interest. It means knowing I have something I can offer to people who need it, and then doing the practical things to make it happen. In the past few years, my service has meant mentoring people who are met with sudden, life threatening disabilities, like spinal cord injuries. It has also meant speaking countless times before high school and college groups about personal responsibility and the risks of drinking and driving. What I also learned is that it has filled me with a joy I hadn't fully understood. It has meant making a difference in somebody's life, even if I didn't always know whom that person was. It has meant sometimes giving tough love, and always giving encouragement. Mostly, it has meant being part of something bigger than myself.

My wife, Tamika Owens, and I fell in love after my accident. The fact that I was paralyzed in a wheelchair did not deter her from loving me. Although Tamika witnessed my life being turned upside down, her love for me remained intact. We were married on November 17, 2007 in front of a packed church. Our love remains strong today. Tamika says, "There's truly something special about Dwight that I can't put into words. He always manages to make me smile even during my angriest moments. I just feel a sense of peace when I am with him. He's truly an inspiration to my life and I thank God for him." I love Tamika for those words and for who she is. She supports my mission; always understanding and never treating me as if I'm handicapped. When I'm in her presence, I still feel like I'm walking and standing tall. On December 12, 2012, Tamika and I welcomed a beautiful daughter, Brailey Samara Owens. Brailey fills my heart with joy daily and motivates me even more to continue bringing inspiration and smiles to other people.

> Service keeps me grounded, humble, and reminds me to be thankful for the small things in life.

For the first year after my accident, my life was centered on survival – both physical and emotional. After two years of multiple surgeries, life-threatening setbacks, and finally a grueling rehabilitation regimen, I emerged with an unwavering resolution in my heart. I was determined to make it all count for something and AmeriCorps helped me do that. I decided to share my story and bring hope to others with disabilities. I remain determined to let the world know that a disability is not a death sentence. I can do anything anyone else can do; I'm just sitting down while doing it. It's that spirit and resolve that brought me to the world of inspirational and motivational speaking. I share my story with tens of thousands, offering the lessons I've learned to the world at large, letting my infectious joy and humor uplift the hopeless.

AmeriCorps truly helped give me a new motivation and purpose. Service keeps me grounded, humble, and reminds me to be thankful for the small things in life. Despite my circumstances, I wake up every morning with unbelievable joy because I'm here to see another day. Despite the wheelchair and paralysis, I am *Still Standing*. I want people to feed off my joy and realize life's value.

DWIGHT R OWENS continues to inspire others as a motivational speaker and author of "Still Standing." For more information on his story, his mission, or to book him for speaking engagements please visit his website at www.StillStandingWithDwight.com.

Oregon, With Love

By **Kathryn deBros**

* Names have been changed

Served in an AmeriCorps State Program with
Partnerships for Student Achievement
Forest Grove, Oregon

My time spent in service to my community was an accidental lesson in expectation. I served from 2007-2008 in the Partnerships for Student Achievement program in Forest Grove, Oregon. In hindsight, it was one of the most meaningful and fulfilling years of my adult life. While I have the luxury of reflecting back on it, I can heartily recommend every young person set aside some time to serve. However, at the time my service didn't feel so great. In fact it felt like a daily boxing match. I was challenged physically, mentally, emotionally and financially, but was encouraged to greet these daily trials head-on and with joy. I learned I am very frequently wrong, but that it's okay. More importantly, I learned it's not what one does, but how one does it.

I arrived in Oregon in August of 2007 expecting a teaching job to be handed to me because of my new teaching license. I had graduated at the top of my class the previous May and was one month into my marriage. I was rather overconfident in my ability to achieve what I desired from the world – and the world's willingness to grant me my

> **More importantly, I learned it's not what one does, but how one does it.**

desires. We had not yet found an apartment and were staying on a futon in my friend's mom's basement when September rolled around. I realized schools generally don't hire after the start of the year. At some point during a frustrated phone call with my mom, she mentioned she thought my cousin had settled in Portland and suggested I give him a call. We hadn't seen each other in 10 years, so I didn't expect him to have any interest in getting a beer with someone he had met only a handful of times. I quickly learned not to underestimate the ability of a Portland microbrewery to bring people together. As I sat with my cousin and his wife, some of his friends biked in from the surrounding Portland area. To my amazement, my cousin's friends were interested in my employment troubles. Not only did they seem to care, they had a solution. One of the biking friends had just begun her second year of service in AmeriCorps working in the school system. While my "maybe…" was still ringing in my ears, the rest happened quickly. Soon I was interviewing in five different schools with five different administrators who all had a twinkle of desperation in their eyes for cheap, educated labor. For my part, I'm not sure I've ever felt so needed.

> " Tutoring is tutoring, but offering school help with inspiration, respect, and love is something else entirely. "

My expectations of grim drudgery were soon allayed when I accepted a position with Partnerships for Student Achievement, in a polished, sunny and optimistic upper-elementary school. I settled into an office in a sunny library. My mentor was the librarian, a woman as warm and caring as any mother, but way cooler. She had rockin' long red hair and a way of fluttering her eyelashes that sent waves of love in your direction. Her reading recommendations for kids were consistently dead on. It was an incredible talent, really. She, like many others I encountered during that year, performed her tasks with joy and flair elevating them beyond the ordinary. The library was a pleasurable place to be for everybody, even those who didn't enjoy reading.

Partnerships for Student Achievement is a program devoted to assisting schools with a high proportion of children below the poverty line and/or at-risk kids. The expectation was to tutor children who struggled in class and develop pre- or post-school groups to help students engage with their classmates and school. We were also responsible for reaching out to parents, recruiting and managing volunteers, and developing service projects to complete on the weekends with fellow volunteers. We also attended a graduate-level class on Thursdays. Additionally, the prior volunteer at my site had run a "Lunch Bunch" group. This was a lunchtime social group helping children who felt alienated positively interact with peers through games and play. Within these parameters, I could fashion the program however I chose. I quickly racked up "clients" as teachers got to know their students. I arranged a "Homework Help" session before school and began a rotating schedule of Lunch Bunch groups. I joined up with the after-school environmental club and created a Book Club. I put up fliers at the local college to find others who were willing to help and put on my best I-Know-What-I'm-Doing face to get them pumped to work with kids.

> Time spent forging a relationship, building trust, and validating is never time wasted, especially with kids who need the bond.

In a nutshell, I was creating positive ways for kids to connect in their own communities with their own peers. Despite their young age, our school struggled with gang involvement, poverty, homelessness, and the agony of feeling different; particularly for Spanish-speaking pre-teens who desperately wanted to fit. The administrators worked hard to make sure school was a safe place for kids. The principal even dressed in a Santa suit and rode into the gym on a pony for the holiday celebration. We were reminded many kids didn't look forward to the vacations because they wouldn't get to eat as frequently. Having a place with consistent routines, expectations and food was vital. Anyone who has worked in a school knows there is much more than academics administered. These kids needed to feel accepted and loved, regardless of their background. I helped provide opportunities for acceptance and love for each individual child.

Mary, a girl whose family had ties to gangs, was pretty and graceful at a point in life where most girls are still awkward. Easily swept up in drama and secrets she could have been attracted to trouble. We met to work on her reading, but ended up talking about whatever was on her mind. Her family was struggling. She had low self-esteem. She essentially wasn't sure what path she wanted to take in life. Her friends would push her to tease others, but she had a streak of kindness. When her friends were whispering about sneaking away from school to take part in something shady, she became alarmed enough to report it to a guidance counselor. Her concern for her friends' safety awarded her Student of the Month. She dressed up neatly, and her whole family arrived for the ceremony to watch her accept the prize. She blushed when a gym full of people applauded enthusiastically for her. We had created a role for her in the school where she felt valued, competent and safe. I don't know what kind of person she will become, but I hope our collective care helped connect her to community so negative influences will be a thing of the past.

> **But small steps are always difficult to see from up close.**

A big part of my work was helping children feel valued in the classroom. Tutoring is tutoring, but offering school help with inspiration, respect, and love is something else entirely. Katie hated school and would stall work together by telling stories about home. When she was frustrated, she would put her head down and stop working. One of our first assignments together was to write a summary of a news story. She would copy the first few sentences of the story and call it done, so I showed her a trick. "Read the whole story, then cover it up. Whatever pops out in your brain is important enough to write down." She agreed to try it, so she read the story silently and said she was ready to summarize. We covered up the newspaper and I watched as she wrote, very carefully, the first few words from the story, exactly as they had been written. Then she looked back at the story and read for a bit, covered it up again, and wrote the next few words...exactly as they had been written.

She slowly progressed from there, but like Mary, Katie and I would talk about more than work. I worried I was wasting precious tutoring time talking, but wasn't disciplined enough to keep our conversations purely academic. At the time I felt guilty, but in the 5 years following my service, I believe this is the best way I helped Katie. Time spent forging a relationship, building trust, and validating is never time wasted, especially with kids who need the bond. Soon, she would smile when I arrived in the doorway of her classroom, her face brightening. She proudly told me how she saw one of her classmates doing summaries the wrong way and taught them how to do it properly.

Katie is one of the best examples I have in my career of the difference motivation makes in accomplishing anything in school and the difference a positive relationship makes in motivation. There was a clear turnaround in her that year; Katie went from putting her head down and ignoring schoolwork to teaching other students how to write. Her classroom behavior improved by raising her hand and asking questions on a regular basis, to debating over which science experiment to do for the science fair. Each science fair category was fascinating to her. Her teacher raved about the difference in attitude. For simplicity's sake and pride's sake, I'm happy to take credit for all of it. However, as any teacher knows, there is precious little we can actually control. I feel fortunate that Katie's willingness and my desire to help came together to build Katie's confidence and curiosity.

My next major revelation came with our monthly service projects. That year was difficult in many ways that need not be recalled. Suffice it to say, waking up early on a Saturday in December to dig giant rhododendrons out of the mud was not high on my list of desirable activities. I was in a particularly foul mood when I

> " AmeriCorps excels at making small steps into huge gains by building a better community. "

arrived at the Oregon Zoo, sipping coffee to build motivation, when I felt like putting my head down like Katie would. We learned we would be working in the bear's cage (with the bear temporarily removed) digging up said rhododendrons while planting new bushes in their place. The zoo employees smirked at us and I couldn't help but think they thought us suckers for agreeing to do this work. They dumped a pile of compost on the ground and smirked some more.

When I saw the field of rhododendrons, I almost died. There were so many. They were so big. It was all full-on, put-your-back-into-it, farm-laborer, start-chewing-tylenol-now sort of work. There was no possible way we were going to be able to finish. No. Freaking. Way. I almost left and went home. Fortunately (or unfortunately), I had too much pride and no other opportunities for employment, so I picked up a shovel and got right into it, digging, pulling, ripping roots apart, and then digging some more. Right when I thought I couldn't dig any more, something amazing happened: I stopped caring. We were all tired and none of us could go anywhere. So we started singing any song which we remembered the words. Some bad songs from the 90s get stuck in your head whether you like them or not. We sang, laughed, joked, and stopped worrying so much about when we would be done.

> In the end, I hope I have given the community as much as it has given me.

During our lunch break, we were free to tour the grounds and visit any of the animals. The best part was at the end of the day, after all the worked was completed; because the smirking zoo employees invited us to visit the bear in his holding pen. The bear's name was Bug and he calmly waited behind bars you'd find in a typical cartoon prison. He stretched his giant paws out with what seemed to be banana-sized claws. We fed him fish and admired his strikingly soft eyes, reflecting on how we'd improved his home. More importantly, we reflected on the completion of our impossible task. There was an incredible sense of accomplishment even if the accomplishment was only digging.

> I learned when you let go of preconceived ideas of how life should be the world is full of amazing experiences.

To be fair, there were many days that didn't come with fresh ideas or revelations of any kind. There were weeks that didn't feel rewarding. But small steps are always difficult to see from up close. In retrospect, AmeriCorps excels at making small steps into huge gains by building a better community. Whether it's planting rhododendrons or chatting with a student who doesn't feel connected at school, AmeriCorps volunteers seem to have mastered not only the what, but the how of building community. I have never met a group of people who perform such seemingly small tasks with so much joy. I felt we were spreading goodwill to our community not just because we were performing kind and helpful actions, but because we were performing them wholeheartedly and singing all the while. And while we spent a great deal of time beautifying the community and helping kids connect, I think the biggest impact was spreading positive energy throughout the community.

In the end, I hope I have given the community as much as it has given me. I learned kids can be naturally curious and motivated if learning is carefully facilitated by someone they trust. I cherish my conversations with students and am honored by the confidence they show when they trust me with their life stories. In my current work with emotionally disturbed students, the relationship is sometimes the only tool with which I have to work. I learned small steps lead to big accomplishments and anyone is capable of small steps. I still look at difficult tasks and think of those damned rhododendrons. I learned manual labor can feel really, really good. I learned when you let go of preconceived ideas of how life should be the world is full of amazing experiences.

KATHRYN DEBROS M.S., works as a special education teacher in rural Vermont, specializing in children with difficult behaviors. Outside of school, she does some freelance writing. She can be reached at Kathryn.debros@gmail.com.

Service is Lifelong

By Gwendolyn Morris

Served with SeniorCorps Alachua County
Foster Grandparent Program
Gainesville, Florida

My name is Gwendolyn Morris and I am 67 years old. I served in a Foster Grandparent Program, which is part of Senior Corps, within AmeriCorps. The Foster Grandparent program affords a way for volunteers over the age of 55 to stay active and engaged in their communities by serving children and youth through reading, mentoring, tutoring and other programs. I served in a Foster Grandparent program located out of Alachua County in Gainesville, Florida.

My job as a Foster Grandparent has had a profound impact on my life. I worked in a school where I helped read to and mentor children in kindergarten. Before I was able to go into the classroom to support schoolchildren, my program provided all of the Foster Grandparents trainings to teach us how to successfully interact with students. It was important we received training before going into classrooms, because we needed to be prepared to properly work with the students in our new roles. Some of the grandparents were assigned to Day Care Centers and others were assigned to schools. The classroom I was chosen for had a first year teacher. She was very young, but she was excellent at her career. All of the children loved her and she went out of her way to connect with the students. Not only did her students learn a lot during their year, but she taught me as well. Her work ethic and dedication were an inspiration.

I learned something new from her and the students everyday. Though I worked with everyone in the class, there were two students in particular I was able to spend a substantial amount of time mentoring and helping throughout the year.

The daily activities in the school varied but I was in the classroom primarily to assist the teacher so she was able to do her job more diligently. I was happy to support the teacher in whatever area was needed, especially when it came to helping individual students with specific areas. To encourage student success, my work included everything from helping with reading, writing, spelling, math, and sometimes coloring assignments for fun. This program and opportunity were not only important to me but the students were also helped and grateful for the extra support. Many children did not have grandparents that lived close, so my colleagues and I served as surrogate grandparents while helping to improve students' learning outcomes. I was so proud whenever I was able to walk the hallways at school because I would be bombarded with little ones yelling, "Hey Grandma"! These memories still make me feel so special!

> Being in the school helped remind me how important adults are in a child's life, especially parents.

Being in the school helped remind me how important adults are in a child's life, especially parents. Parents are a child's first teacher and they have a responsibility to shape their child's world. Since becoming a Foster Grandparent, I have encouraged my own children to read to my grandchildren more, because I see the importance of this skill development. It is essential for parents to interact with their children every day, especially through reading. To supplement the work parents do with their children, teachers and Foster Grandparents can also work to cultivate and build on the skills children need to succeed in life. I hope the work I completed in the classroom was able to fill even small gaps in the student's lives. Since working as a Foster Grandparent, I have been reminded of my first grade teacher and the significance of school. I can still remember my first grade classroom, even after all this time. More importantly, I remember the stories I read, the same stories that I now read to my students. *See Jane Run, Jack and Jill,* and *Jack and the Beanstalk* are all stories I have told over and over again.

One of the many other amazing aspects of my job as a Foster Grandparent was to be able to go on field trips with the children. These outside classroom learning opportunities provided much needed experience for the students. It is so critical for a child to become familiar with the outdoors and the outside world in addition to their classroom education. One of the most fun field trips we would take was to the library. Public libraries are fundamental because they are free and open to all. If children visit the library they have the potential to develop a love for reading that can last a lifetime. This is such a significant skill set for children to have so they are able to become successful later on in life. The library can also teach children secondary skills through the many extracurricular classes they offer. Children can learn to sing, speak in public, listen to others, interact with other children, keep quiet, write, and most importantly how to read. Field trips were exhilarating chances for the students and myself to learn while out in the community.

> "To supplement the work parents do with their children, teachers and Foster Grandparents can also work to cultivate and build on the skills children need to succeed in life."

On top of the remarkable opportunities I was able to have in the classroom, the Foster Grandparent program also provided ways for me to improve my own life and skill sets. We had in-service days once a month that helped us learn about different things that may be affecting our day-to-day lives. My entire cohort has learned from different speakers about subjects like elder abuse, health fairs available in our area, Medicare, child abuse, healthy eating habits, the importance of active living and exercise, and diabetes education. These in-service days provided me with valuable information allowing me to take better care of students and myself. The program also gave my colleagues and I the opportunity to participate in different activities together. We attended bingo nights, exercise classes, talent shows, round table discussions on various topics and rock-a-thons. These were awesome events and we also had the privilege of hosting special events like the Valentine's social. We were able to invite family and friends, so that they could learn about the amazing Foster Grandparent program. The Valentine's social especially was a great success and I was excited to share my work with the important people in my life.

> If every child had access to these resources, especially those kids that need love and extra attention, then the world would be a better place.

When I first learned about the Foster Grandparent program I was skeptical and nervous. I am so thankful to my family and friends who encouraged me to become a Foster Grandparent. The program has allowed me to learn so much from my peers and through the facilitators and trainers. I am so appreciative to be a part of this remarkable program. It has brought great joy to my life and reminds me how imperative it is to still give back at my age. I am able to have a lasting impact in the lives of students, especially those that need extra care and attention. I can truly say I wish the Foster Grandparent program was available in every school in America, as well as every school in the world. If every child had access to these resources, especially those kids that need love and extra attention, then the world would be a better place. If young students received proper nurturing early on they would be prepared to continue on in school to become successful. Anyone who is a Foster Grandparent can offer love and joy to students and they can teach them how to pass it on to others around them every single day. This program has changed my life and Alachua County is a better because it exists.

GWENDOLYN MORRIS has been a volunteer with Alachua County Foster Grandparent Program for two years in Gainesville, Florida. In her spare time she enjoys helping children in her community and church as well as being a mother to three children and a grandmother to four grandchildren.

Amending the Path

. . . .

By **Andrea Shultice**

* Names have been changed

Served in AmeriCorps State and National with Community
Building Partnerships for Youth in Transition at CBPYT at the
Denver Department of Human Services Chafee Program &
The Boys & Girls Club of Fremont County
Denver, Colorado & Canon City, Colorado

Service and volunteerism have always been part of my life, mostly through church and school. "National service" more specifically became a full-time endeavor when I joined AmeriCorps right out of college in 2010. Though I had lived my whole life up to that point in Iowa, I had a love of travel and a flair for adventure in my spirit. So I accepted a position at the Department of Human Services (DHS) in Denver, Colorado, without ever having set foot (or knowing a soul) in the city.

This was also a completely new direction for me, because even though I considered myself a service-minded person, all of my professional training and experience up to that point was much more academic in nature than anything resembling social work. I majored in English and History with a minor in Mathematics. I wanted to go on to graduate school in Latin American History so I could one day be a professor at a small, liberal arts school like Simpson College, from which I had just graduated. I saw AmeriCorps as a perfect "gap year" experience—it would give me a break from school, experience in a new area, and, most importantly, it

. . . .

would be meaningful work. My family hosted a few different exchange students over the years while I was growing up, and a few of them went on to mandatory national service for their own respective country for a year or more—some via the military, others in domestic civil service. I always admired this standard of citizenship and felt it important to devote myself full-time for at least a year of my life to my own nation. Additionally, I was raised in the Church of Jesus Christ of Latter-day Saints, so I held (and still hold) a deep-seated notion that Christ-like service to others is fundamentally important to my Heavenly Father, and therefore necessary in my own life.

All of these things, plus a desire to live near the mountains during my first period of true independence, logically led me to the DHS position in Denver. The particular DHS division I served in was called Chafee, which provided caseworkers and resources to youth aged 16-21, who were currently in or transitioning out of foster care. Chafee's goal was to help smooth these kids' transition to independence. Chafee caseworkers taught 16-week "Independent Living" classes, that met at least once a month if not more. Each case worker had roughly 40 kids on their caseload and acted as professional advocates alongside the kids' regular caseworkers (for those still in foster care), school counselors, guardians *ad litem*, foster parents, kinship, birth family members, therapists, and so on. My job was two-fold: to join this team of adults who tried desperately to fill the impossibly large void left by the kids' parents and to mentor a caseload of 10-12 Chafee youth under the direction of one of the Chafee caseworkers.

To be clear, all logic and details aside, this absolutely terrified me. As a small-town Iowa girl who wanted to be a college professor, serving inner-city foster teens—some of whom were not that much younger than me—and trying to help them achieve independent, living-related goals while still trying to become independent myself, with absolutely no education or experience in this area, seemed a tad overwhelming. I was not sure I was tough enough to handle the issues I knew these kids faced, which made me feel insecure about my ability to do much good. But previous experience with service (such as fixing rooftops as part of hurricane relief efforts in Texas and teaching a creative writing course to inmates at a women's prison) had taught me that with hard work and good training, going outside my comfort zone to serve others yielded powerful results. So I packed up and moved out to Denver.

When I first started my job, I immediately entered student mode. I memorized the myriad acronyms associated with social services. I attended all trainings offered by DHS that seemed remotely relevant to my position, I read a bunch of books, and I tried to soak in all the knowledge I could from my hilarious supervisor. When I started getting clients of my own, I was still basically a nervous wreck. On a number of occasions, I questioned the effectiveness, not only of

> " But previous experience with service (such as fixing rooftops as part of hurricane relief efforts in Texas and teaching a creative writing course to inmates at a women's prison) had taught me that with hard work and good training, going outside my comfort zone to serve others yielded powerful results. "

my own work, but also of the entire AmeriCorps model, as it seemed I wasn't the only one in my corps struggling with the same issues. Most of us moved to Denver for this job, many had not studied or worked in social work before, and we were all serving "youth in transition" at schools, in government agencies, or through nonprofits. All of our youth were considered "at risk" for one reason or another. We worked with foster youth, teen parents, low-income kids, refugees, homeless youth, addicts, delinquents, and others. With issues this serious, how much long-term change could we really effect during our eleven-month term?

In these early moments of doubt, and many times since, I have recalled the words a college friend who studied social work told me before I left for Denver. She said, more or less, "In social work, we very rarely get to see the consequences of our hard work. It's easy to feel like you're failing or that you just don't know what you're doing, but don't worry. Your work affects people. Years later, someone will think of something you said and it will cause him or her to make a change you thought would never come. You won't be there to see it, but that doesn't make it any less real or your work from before any less essential." This sort of advice may seem obvious to some, but in my most frustrating, heartbreaking moments, her words brought me comfort and strength. At the beginning of my first year of national service, this strength helped me get over my insecurities and worries that I wasn't qualified and just do my job the best I could.

Luckily, at least a few of the youth I mentored were completely receptive to my role in their lives. One such girl, Cecile, was dead set on going to college out of state, but had never actually been on a college visit. I helped organize a visit to Colorado State University (CSU) in Fort Collins. She fell in love with the campus, and she's now a junior there and loving it. In all fairness to Cecile—this girl was going to succeed in life, whether or not she met me. However, it may not have been at CSU. And I think she likes her life there. This taught me that even for those whose life trajectories are most definitely headed upward, positive role models can still make a difference.

Another girl I mentored, Jacqueline, has one of the softest hearts of anyone I've ever met. If you met her, you would never believe that she had endured unimaginable trauma as a young teen. She was, however, definitely a girl who needed—and wanted—someone to help give her direction in life. This made our relationship mutually beneficial. We met once a week (or more) for over 10 months. We trudged through the slow and sometimes painful process of learning to budget. One of my biggest AmeriCorps successes is knowing that by the time I completed my year of service, Jacqueline no longer qualified for food stamps because she had too much money in her bank account. This is obviously due to her hard work and commitment, but also to the time I spent with her. On Valentine's Day, Jacqueline gave me a gift bag filled with lotion, fuzzy socks, and bubble bath. I thanked her and told her that she really did not need to get me anything, and her response still makes me smile: "Oh please, Andie! You deserve it, and you know I got more money than you anyway!" And she was absolutely right. (I still qualified for food stamps myself.) I was blessed to be there for most of Jacqueline's

> " This taught me that even for those whose life trajectories are most definitely headed upward, positive role models can still make a difference. "

biggest moments that year—high school graduation, her first college visit, college registration, and her first hike in the Rockies.

The most paradoxical part of working with foster youth was the conflicting joy and sorrow I felt at getting to be so close with these kids for so many important and meaningful moments, but only because in some cases they had literally no one else in the world to be there. Jacqueline signed the paperwork to give me access to her college grades because she thought I was the only one who would care enough to check in and get on her if she fell behind.

> Jacqueline taught me programs like AmeriCorps work because there are people out there who want someone to care enough to show up and to put in the time.

It didn't matter to her that I had almost no training in how to work with traumatized teens. For her, I was a young woman she admired and she felt the love I had for her. She saw me show up every time I said I was going to, even though I was usually ten minutes late. She trusted me enough to take my advice and when it worked for her, she trusted me even more. Jacqueline taught me programs like AmeriCorps work because there are people out there who want someone to care enough to show up and to put in the time. If Jacqueline didn't have anyone to be her mentor at that time in life, she would not have made the transition to independence quite so happily or successfully. My position mattered, very concretely, to her.

As for my own life, I decided to serve a second term with AmeriCorps, this time a couple hours south of Denver at a Boys & Girls Club in Cañon City. This position brought a whole new set of challenges, as it was a new club in a very small city. I was in charge of creating and implementing educational programs at our club, in addition to a long list of other random duties the staff shared, as we tried to establish ourselves with the teens and the community. Without going into too many details, my second year in national service caused me to grow in completely new ways. The one thing it had in common with my year at DHS was it further cemented in me a love for teens, "especially those who need us most," as the Boys & Girls Club slogan goes.

Now that these two experiences are over, I see the legacy of national service still permeates my day-to-day thoughts. First and foremost, I married a man I met from Simpson who also served in AmeriCorps. Also a lifelong Iowan, he moved out to Washington (state) and worked at a small, rural school district in the valley near Mt. Rainier. In college he majored in Economics and Philosophy, and initially viewed his year with AmeriCorps similar to how I did—as a gap year that is both meaningful and adventurous, but likely unrelated to his overall career trajectory. Nevertheless, he allowed his experience to transform his life path. He is now nearing the completion of his Teach for America (TFA) service. TFA is a national organization that helps prospective teachers get their degree in teaching by providing them a discounted education, a teacher's income, full-time experience, and teaching licensure in exchange for two years of full-time teaching in the nation's toughest schools. In a few months, Blake will be certified to teach elementary school and will have his Masters in Education from Marquette University in Milwaukee, Wisconsin. I have been so proud and honored to know him through this entire process. Much of why we chose to marry one another is because of the shared values that led us to, and were cultivated by, our experiences with national service. We both feel deeply committed to a life of service, in the many forms we know it will take as our lives unfold together.

> Now that these two experiences are over, I see the legacy of national service still permeates my day-to-day thoughts.

I am currently in my second year of graduate school; in a few months I will earn a Masters in Global History from Marquette. Though full-time service is not so obviously present in this current life chapter its impact is still supremely influential. Without my AmeriCorps experiences, I never would have considered taking a break between MA and Ph.D. programs to teach at a community college or on staff at a small college or university to serve first-generation or ESL college students. These comprise the bulk of the applications I am putting out as I prepare to enter the job market. AmeriCorps gave me greater awareness of other possible careers I would love and I am much more open to amending "the path" I had set out for myself so it more intentionally includes service to teens and young adults who might need someone like me.

ANDREA SHULTICE recently finished a Master of Arts in Global History at Marquette University in Milwaukee, Wisconsin. She plans to spend a few years serving first generation college students at a small liberal arts college in Iowa before returning to school to earn her Ph.D. in Latin American History, with hopes of teaching at a small college someday.

A Sense of Belonging

By Avery Olmstead

Served in an AmeriCorps State and National program
with Born to Read and Project GOALS (Go Online
with AmeriCorps at Libraries and Schools)
Maine Statewide

Really, my journey as an AmeriCorps Member began by accident. In 1999, I was at a crossroads in my life. I had graduated from college five years earlier but gainful employment was proving elusive. As a person who uses a wheelchair, I was finding the job market harder than I had expected. At that point in my life, I was pretty discouraged. One day I happened to see an ad in the local paper for someone to read at local daycare centers and nursery schools. This wasn't what I had specialized in, but it sounded really interesting. It was something I was confident I could do successfully.

At the interview, I found out it was an AmeriCorps position. As it turned out, I hadn't read the ad completely. Unfortunately, I knew nothing about AmeriCorps. So, I did the only thing I could do, ask. After learning more about the program, I was intrigued. Honestly, I was also interested in the educational reward. I knew at some point I was going to further my education, but I had no idea how to pay for it. I saw AmeriCorps as a way to have an impact and accomplish that goal at the same time.

I was fortunate enough to pass the interview. I was excited, but also nervous. I am a very strong person and someone who enjoys meeting new people. However, in work situations, I used to be anxious because I was unsure if people would accept me or think I was a burden to have around. I found out quickly how accepted I would feel.

> However, in work situations, I used to be nervous because I was unsure if people would accept me or think I was a burden to have around. I found out quickly how accepted I would feel.

The job I had applied for was offered statewide. Several of us were accepted into the program. Before we started our assignments, we were asked to attend a two-day training. The evening before training began, my Personal Care Assistant called and explained they could not take the job. Considering I was already at the training and my family was two hours away, I started to panic. My new colleagues asked me what was wrong and when I told them, it was as if I had instantly gained a bunch of friends. They told me not to worry, that everything was going to be okay and that they were glad I was there. My co-workers took it upon themselves to inform our project director what was going on and he generously offered to help me for the weekend. I was so touched by all of this because even though my family was extremely supportive, I had grown up feeling I had to apologize to the world for having a disability and the unique challenges that often brings. I found out that evening just how much people accepted me and I didn't have to hide to be accepted by my peers.

I also learned so much from the actual job. I realized very quickly I had a unique opportunity to talk about disability issues just by being myself. Every new place I went,

> The best way to break down fear and to bust stereotypes is to communicate with each other.

kids asked me how my chair worked, if they could push it, if they could touch it. They asked me why I was in the chair and would tell of a friend or relative also in a chair. I loved the fact the kids didn't have a filter. I enjoyed how they asked me anything that popped into their heads. It bothers me when people, especially adults, are afraid to talk or ask questions. The best way to break down fear and to bust stereotypes is to communicate with each other. I wish people would ask me questions about my wheelchair instead of being afraid of me or ignoring me. As a society, we are all better served when kids are exposed to differences at an early age.

Near the end of the first service year, I was asked to speak at a conference on disability issues for AmeriCorps. Not only was it a great honor, but through that, I was asked to apply for another service position. My confidence boosted because for the first time in my life that I was pursued for a position. My second AmeriCorps year involved working at local libraries where I gave lessons to patrons on how to use the internet. Again, I felt like I was accepted by my peers from the beginning and felt like I had as much to bring to the table. My most vivid memory of that year is a beautiful one. After completing lessons over a few months with a local woman in my hometown, I received a handwritten note from her saying because of our time together, she felt like she had the confidence to go back to school and finish her degree. That moved me. In life, it's pretty rare to get direct feedback on how someone's life changed because of your actions. If I'm having a bad day, thinking about that note makes me feel better.

> " feeling comfortable in my skin is something I'm still working on, but I'm light-years ahead of where I used to be. I truly believe AmeriCorps was part of that transformation. "

As I stated earlier, my initial reason for joining AmeriCorps was for the educational reward. I never thought my experience would boost my self-confidence and help change me as a person. I'll be honest, feeling comfortable in my skin is something I'm still working on, but I'm light-years ahead of where I used to be. I truly believe AmeriCorps was part of that transformation. Oh, and I did further my education. I spent so much time in libraries during my time in AmeriCorps that I ended up obtaining a Masters in Library & Information Science.

AVERY OLMSTEAD earned a Masters of Library & Information Science in 2008 from the University of South Carolina. He will soon be completing a 2.5 year stint as an Independent Librarian Consultant for the Department of Disability and Human Development at the University of Illinois - Chicago. Avery's next goal is to figure out whether he wants to work towards being a law librarian, public librarian or public policy analyst. Email: averyolmstead@gmail.com

The Power of Continued Service

By **Erin Busk**

Served in an AmeriCorps State Program with Neighborhood
After School Corps & Served in Public Allies
Indianapolis, Indiana

The journey I started through National Service was very sudden. However, the motivation of service and understanding of community were introduced to me early in life—serving as a foundation for me to build upon as an adult. After taking a leap of faith into the world of service, my life molded into meaning—propelling me into a career, a passion, a life-long movement.

The Beginning

I was born into a strong, resilient community, spanning diversity in all forms. My community invested in helping shape my character, my education and most of my entire path to adulthood. It was in my early years that I was infused with a sense of community in its purest form—achieving meaning, sustainability, and happiness through relationships.

There were defining moments in my childhood that first introduced how community and service were connected. All areas that were deficit in my life were compensated by those around me, serving as mentors, teachers, and friends. By witnessing the service of others, I began to see my ability to serve, developing a fire, burning with passion for my community.

As time passed, had I known that what was being infused in my soul would play such a large role in creating the woman I am today—I may have been more apt to delve deeper and deeper into the benefits and service of those around me. The idea of service never left my realm of interest. I always saw the longevity of my community as a passing of a baton, taking lessons of service from those around me and passing it on those younger and in most need.

The Transition

In the later years of my first round of college, I was dumbfounded as to what I was actually going to do after graduation hit. Applying for AmeriCorps was the first step in a life of service—potentially helping me create a better world for youth. Getting to this point was a slow, uphill battle between paying the bills and finding purpose.

The Journey Begins

I accepted my first term of service with AmeriCorps State (Neighborhood After School Corps) in May 2010. I was placed within a local Boys and Girls Club, running programs with school-aged kids. Suddenly thrown into the world of youth service, I quickly discovered it would take more than a passion for service to make a difference—it would require abundant understanding and motivation in order to really serve directly.

During my first few months I was able to have space to learn more about my community and myself and what both were capable of and willing to do for the greater good. I learned about the importance of "serving" instead of "working" for AmeriCorps. I attended training, team building activities, staff meetings, which all complimented the service-oriented foundation I had within me.

After a brief summer term, I accepted a second term with the

Neighborhood After School Corps. I spent the next school year getting to know the kids I worked with; what their lives were like, what their dreams were, what they wanted to do for their community. It wasn't until that winter that I realized I had been given an opportunity to infuse service into their lives as well. Without the efforts of my own community, my challenges growing up would not have propelled me into a life of service. It was those around me that took time to show me the power of people uniting and what "banding together" really meant for the prosperity of community. Being able to show children within my programs this same thing was the highlight of my time with them.

> " I learned about the importance of "serving" instead of "working" for AmeriCorps. "

Public Allies

Once again faced with the end of a journey, I was lost as to what to do with all of this energized, organized motivation. How do I continue to serve youth in a positive way? What careers would allow me the opportunity to show the power of service to kids? After hearing of Public Allies and its strong convictions of collaboration and grassroots community development, I was hooked.

> " I saw how service through Public Allies generated capacity and taught inclusion, how spreading the message of national service left lasting impressions on neighbors and professionals alike. "

I began my third and final term of service with Public Allies Indianapolis in September 2011. I was placed with the Girl Scouts of Central Indiana and put in charge of setting up and executing direct programming with youth within public housing in Indianapolis. My time with Public Allies truly changed my life. I was shown community from a totally new viewpoint, how service and relationships build something powerful, how resources combined serve as a means of survival, happiness and create a thriving community.

I was taught professional skills and learned the interworking of an international nonprofit organization; I witnessed how tradition seeps into the core of families—creating a bond between organizations and neighbors. I saw how service through Public Allies generated capacity and taught inclusion, how spreading the message of national service left lasting impressions on neighbors and professionals alike.

> **Without Public Allies, I would not have developed myself past the point of motivation and into the point of mobilization.**

Public Allies focused on developing the person as much as the program, targeting self-discovery and personal development. I learned about my strengths: adaptability, positivity, and connectedness. I learned about my challenges: long-term planning, idea creation, and execution. I built strong relationships that were rooted in service, civic responsibility and love for neighbors.

Without Public Allies, I would not have developed myself past the point of motivation and into the point of mobilization. The program generated a sense of purpose and passion—in order to help communities create sustainable change within themselves. Through the team service project I learned community, in its broadest form, is still bound by a foundation in love, service and sustainability. Without Public Allies, my commitment to service and grassroots change would have been under-developed and under-utilized.

Post-AmeriCorps

After Public Allies ended, I stayed with my placement organization, Girl Scouts of Central Indiana, where I was promoted and oversaw five key areas. I also oversaw a program within the Indiana Women's prison and a program working with foster care youth. I have since accepted a position with my first AmeriCorps placement, the Boys and Girls Clubs of Indianapolis—as an Evening Reporting Center (ERC) Program

Director. I oversee case management, curriculum, and mentoring of teens affected by the juvenile justice system. I am an active alumni of Public Allies Indianapolis and am working on completing a Master's degree in Public Affairs, focusing on Public Policy.

I attribute my success, personally, professionally, and educationally, to the skills I learned during my time with AmeriCorps and Public Allies. They both allowed me to develop as a person, neighbor, and peer. Their presence in my life continually fuels my passion for service.

Without the opportunity to participate in national service, I don't know where I would be. I can't say for certain—but I can say with confidence, that my professional skills, community commitment and immersion into service would be diluted. My love for my community would be manifested in hope and not in tangible action.

Service is at the core of my career, my educational pursuits, and my community efforts. I continue to work on enhancing my strengths and challenges. I continue to work with youth, in order to fuel their passion for their community. I continue to pursue service in all aspects of my life. This holistic approach is attributed to the development I received within national service. Addressing service from the body, soul, spirit, gets to the root of service and its importance in development of relationships. Above all, national service connected me to other people just as eager to be engaged and see communities thrive.

> " Service is at the core of my career, my educational pursuits, and my community efforts. "

Without service, I would be unfulfilled.
Without service, we lose sight of righteousness.
Without service, communities will suffer.

ERIN BUSK is currently pursuing her Masters in Public Affairs in Public Policy at Indiana University School of Public and Environmental Affairs in Indianapolis. She is also working in the nonprofit field, managing and mentoring teens affected by the juvenile justice system. To contact: erin.busk@yahoo.com

Waking Up

By **Caitlin Closser**

Served in an AmeriCorps National Program
with Rebuilding Together CapacityCorps
Dayton, Ohio

any years ago I served in AmeriCorps. Though that is when my involvement in service began, it is by no means where it has ended. AmeriCorps has been a substantial part of my story for a long time. I am a different person because of it and remain indebted to the influence it still has on my life today.

At the end of 2008, my life shifted. The educational publishing company where I'd been working since graduating college abruptly and rather unapologetically closed their doors, informing us in an email that we had all lost our jobs. There had been no warning and there was very little explanation, other than to blame the poor economy.

> **Many years ago I served in AmeriCorps. Though that is when my involvement in service began, it is by no means where it has ended.**

However, as surreal and unsettling as the situation was, I had to admit I was kind of excited. Upon graduating and entering full time into the adult world, I had naively assumed that by this point in my life I would know what I wanted to do. Though my early career had provided me with a steady paycheck and legitimate business experience, it had also fostered a growing sense of disillusionment.

I don't think I quite had words for it, but I knew I struggled with the values of corporate America, particularly its relentless profit-at-all-costs drive. In the grand scheme of things, I took comfort that educational publishing wasn't such a heartless evil, but it still felt empty. Wasn't there more to life than this?

When I lost my job, I realized I had been given a second chance to find greater satisfaction in my career. Perhaps I could switch to something completely new. Perhaps I could do better this time around.

Unfortunately, my initial optimism quickly wilted.

In early 2009, as the entire country began to slip into The Great Recession, jobs were increasingly difficult to secure and my location certainly didn't help. My hometown, Dayton, OH, where I was living at the time, had most recently suffered a disproportionate blow from the American auto industry's fiscal troubles. As a shrinking city planted firmly in the country's so-called "rust belt", Dayton had already been experiencing a hemorrhaging population loss and the flight of major employers from the region for decades. I'd grown up in the midst of that desolation with only a vague sense of what it meant.

Now, as a true job seeker for the first time, (in full disclosure, my first job had stemmed from an internship the previous summer) I understood the gravity of the situation. Scanning job boards, I saw only a scant few positions I was interested in and quickly realized I wasn't qualified for any of them.

I vented my frustration to friends, which led to one of them suggesting AmeriCorps. When I scanned my memory, I realized I'd vaguely heard that name, but didn't really know what it was about.

As a result, sometime during those bleak winter months, I found myself on AmeriCorps's website where I discovered exactly what I was looking for. There were so many opportunities! They were all over the country, working in all kinds of different fields. It was a gold mine.

Sorting through the various offerings, I soon determined I would only look in Dayton. My life was well established; there were plenty of things keeping me there. To be honest, the abundance of options was a little overwhelming without some guardrails. There were four different positions in Dayton and I applied to all of them. Though I was concerned about the tiny living stipend, I had supports in place. I'd already been maintaining a second, part-time job for the past couple years.

So I went for it.

The position I ended up choosing was an Outreach Coordinator with Rebuilding Together Dayton. I was to be a member of the CapacityCorps program of Rebuilding Together, a national nonprofit that performs home repairs at no cost to the low-income, elderly and disabled homeowners who live in them. In repairing homes, they enable the elderly to age in place and help prevent foreclosures. This helps revitalize neighborhoods and strengthen communities. The office in Dayton is one of over 200 affiliates across the nation.

Plus, the program's orientation was to take place in New Orleans. Having never visited the Crescent City, I can't say that the trip didn't influence my decision.

Since Hurricane Katrina, Rebuilding Together had maintained a strong presence in New Orleans. They had committed to help at the beginning and resolved to stay and help even as other aid grew leaner over the years.

I looked forward to orientation all summer.

Though harboring expectations can lead to disappointment, my experiences exceeded any I could have imagined. I learned so much, was challenged to think about issues I hadn't ever considered in depth, and met one of the most incredible groups of people I have ever had the pleasure of befriending.

Orientation mostly meant classroom-style discussions and team building activities, but also featured events like a scavenger hunt through New Orleans' famed French Quarter. A day of service gave everyone a taste of the kind of work Rebuilding Together performs.

One of the most moving experiences was after our project day, when staff members from the New Orleans affiliate joined our 15-passenger vans to guide us on a tour of the Ninth Ward. As is commonly known, the Ninth Ward is one of the lowest-income neighborhoods in the city and also one of the greatest sites of destruction from Hurricane Katrina and its ensuing flood. Seeing it for the first time was a sobering experience.

Nearly four years after the storm, the evidence of destruction still remaining was staggering. Houses had collapsed in on themselves; gouged with holes and choked in weedy overgrowth. Other plots were void of any house at all. Often everything above the concrete foundation and stoop were washed away, leaving only the skeleton of what was once a home. We were told that people who grow up in New Orleans tend to stay; most families had been in the same home for generations. Houses had been passed down in families for so long everyone had lost track of the deed. If having a home passed down makes it easier to live through poverty, losing it makes it that much harder to rebuild.

It was heartbreaking.

But it was also affirming. Yes, things were bad, but at least I was on the side of the solution. I knew I was on the right track.

Back home, refreshed and excited, I settled in to my new office. We were small, just three staff and two AmeriCorps members, all cozied into the upstairs of an old house on a local university campus. Conveniently, it was just a few blocks from my house and fairly central to the neighborhoods where we were most active.

Much of the work took place in the office where I helped coordinate projects, volunteers, supplies and other logistics. I located and worked with homeowners throughout Dayton. I also created documents, presentations, and other outreach materials.

I was able to be part of some incredible things. In November, as part of a joint project with our local energy supplier, we helped a homeowner locate and patch a deadly carbon monoxide leak. The family told us they'd been experiencing headaches for a long time, but hadn't known the cause was poisonous gas.

Later that year, for my requisite independent service project, I conducted a storytelling project with some of Rebuilding Together Dayton's past homeowners. I had high school creative writing students (from the school I had also attended) interview them. It was a learning experience and a touching presentation when the students read their finished stories to the homeowners for the first time.

The next spring was dominated by preparation for Rebuilding Day, the annual one-day rebuilding blitz that is the organization's signature event. On the last Saturday in April, across the country, volunteers gather to take on a variety of home rebuilding and renewal projects.

Rebuilding Together Dayton's event featured 35 homes and nearly 1300 volunteers. As you can imagine, the logistics of such an event are mammoth. Fortunately, my experienced affiliate had long ago worked out the kinks and the process now functioned as an impressively efficient machine. Touring some of the project sites that day to help deliver ladders, I experienced a tangible energy from the heartwarming outpouring of kindness and selflessness.

I became addicted to that feeling.

After the dust of Rebuilding Day settled, it was time to prepare for Seasonal Volunteer Program projects. It was my role to run the program, which meant finding/creating projects, gauging how many volunteers they could accommodate for how long, making all necessary preparations and sometimes leading the groups through the project implementation. Over the course of that summer, I led volunteers of all ages through 3500 service hours.

But I still wanted more.

Unfortunately, the nature of AmeriCorps is such that all finite things must end. I'd been able to extend my 11-month commitment a few extra weeks to finish out the summer's projects, but with that point of closure came the reality it was time to find something new.

For a variety of reasons, I'd decided to move to Chicago. I had a housing situation figured out and both friends and family already living in the city. I had done some precursory job searching and the results looked promising.

Shrouded in my own blind optimism, I packed my life into a truck and moved to Chicago on Labor Day in 2010. I finally knew what I was looking for; I had a purpose and a place where it could be fulfilled.

I settled in to the new routine. While my roommate went to work, I rotated to different coffee shops in the neighborhood and spent whole days searching for jobs, writing cover letters, and researching organizations.

No luck. Eventually I took a serving job so I wasn't just hemorrhaging funds.

Six months in, I finally lost hope completely and accepted a position at an advertising agency where I knew a friend. I've been there ever since.

Job search aside, this is not a story of failure. Within my first month or so in Chicago, I'd been connected to two groups that have shaped my life deeply. I met one of the co-founders of the AmeriCorps Alums Chicago chapter. She was also building a network in Chicago for ServeNext, a grassroots organization advocating for national service opportunities. ServeNext has since merged with a similar organization and goes by the name ServiceNation.

I immediately joined both causes, excited to be reconnected to the AmeriCorps world again.

ServeNext's efforts focused mainly on engaging politicians and political candidates in discussions about AmeriCorps and other programs under the Corporation for National and Community Service, a government agency. Sometimes this took the form of scheduled meetings with local government leaders, other times it meant trying to be in the same place at the same time as a candidate to try to elicit a vocal promise of support for national service opportunities.

> And that is where alums come in. As people who know firsthand the value of AmeriCorps, I believe we owe it to future generations to preserve it, to ensure that our children and grandchildren have the same life-changing opportunities we did.

I eventually applied and was accepted to a position as the Field Corps Organizer for ServeNext Chicago, the nascent network that my friend had started a few months prior. It was a part-time appointment, complete with a small stipend. Though it wasn't enough to replace my full-time job, it was validating work.

During my twelve months with ServeNext, I rebuilt a network of local service supporters, met with the offices of Senators and Representatives, promoted several nationwide advocacy days and events, and explained service advocacy to the world.

Most people with a stake in AmeriCorps don't realize just how precarious the program's position is in the Congressional budget. Though national service is generally regarded favorably, when it comes time to make tough budgetary decisions, it is these programs that are often marked for deletion.

And that is where alums come in. As people who know firsthand the value of AmeriCorps, I believe we owe it to future generations to preserve it, to ensure that our children and grandchildren have the same life-changing opportunities we did.

I have integrated this passion into involvement with AmeriCorps Alums Chicago. Since first meeting the co-founding president, I have been actively involved on the Leadership Committee of the organization. We have experienced some turnover, a rotating cast of members and fluctuating energy and participation levels.

> " My term in AmeriCorps was my beginning. Through it, I discovered a whole new part of myself—I woke up to a sense of purpose in life. "

In spite of the challenges, we have accomplished a lot and have been afforded some incredible opportunities. We've coordinated large-scale service projects, networking and leadership development events and maintained engagement with a network of around 800 alums.

Thanks to our affiliation with the AmeriCorps Alums national office, a group of us were invited last year to a meeting at the White House. As part of their Champions of Change event, alums from across the country were invited to be celebrated and to hear more about what the White House administration is doing to further service. It was an incredible, once-in-a-lifetime experience and I feel so fortunate that I was able to be a part of it.

Part of my service has also been to continue with Rebuilding Together. Since completing my term, I've been able to work on several large-scale, national events around the country. I served first in New Orleans, helping repair a home as part of Rebuilding Together's 50 for 5 event, in which 50 homes were repaired in 5 days for the five-year anniversary of Hurricane Katrina. In subsequent years, I volunteered as a House Captain, leading volunteers through project executions in Philadelphia, Nashville, and Columbus, OH. These projects were part of

Rebuilding Together's annual Building a Healthy Neighborhood event, which concentrates on 20-35 homes centered within a few blocks in order to make a bigger impact on the whole neighborhood.

With every event, the collected positivity around serving others creates a warmth unlike anything I've ever experienced.

> I believe the solution to the world's ills is in combatting them with kindness and compassion.

My term in AmeriCorps was my beginning. Through it, I discovered a whole new part of myself—I woke up to a sense of purpose in life. I believe that beginning has enabled me to grow into a more service-oriented, giving and aware person.

I have always been an optimist and as such believe deeply in the great impact that can be made by the combination of small acts. I like to think every instance of helping someone else contributes to a positive energy, and every service project helps perpetuate a spirit of giving. I believe the solution to the world's ills is in combatting them with kindness and compassion.

I like to hope a lifetime spent striving to achieve these ideals will help create something greater than just the life itself.

CAITLIN CLOSSER has parted ways with her aforementioned job in order to transition her career into working full-time in the service sector. She continues to stay engaged with Rebuilding Together and is now leading the AmeriCorps Alums Chicago chapter as President.

AmeriCorps, AmeriPath, AmeriLife

By **Betsy Laakso**

Served as a VISTA with Together We Can Make a
Difference & Volunteer Centers of Michigan
Council Bluffs, Iowa &
Lansing, Michigan

In the spring of 2003 I was entering year three of my first job out of college. I worked for a corporation that was breaking through with new technology and designs. My English degree didn't do much for me in this position, but it was an exciting and quickly growing field. I thought I had done well for myself landing this job right out of college, but soon found I was searching for something more. In my spare time, I started volunteering, seeking every opportunity I could to better my community. I wanted to make a difference, but I didn't have much direction. I simply found ways to volunteer and showed up ready to help.

My job wasn't what made me happy, but what else was there for me to do? I started thinking about the Peace Corps. I looked online and started the application process, when suddenly AmeriCorps started popping up in my online searches. What is this AmeriCorps thing? Without much thought I submitted an application. Michigan was home, but I was up for an adventure. I got calls the next day from Maine, Iowa, and Arizona. I was ready to accept a position in Maine, when the American Red Cross chapter in Council Bluffs, Iowa called me. They told me about their program and made it sound like an amazing opportunity. Suddenly, I had a bigger decision to make. My dad advised me, as father's do, that it wasn't a decision someone else could make for me; I needed to follow my gut. My gut said "Go to Iowa." I accepted the AmeriCorps VISTA position at the Loess Hills Chapter.

I arrived at the Red Cross chapter not knowing where I was going to live; yet so many friendly people greeted me, all excited for me to become part of the team. I made my new home in Omaha, Nebraska with Paige Thomas. As I soon found out, it wasn't unusual for someone like Paige to open their home and quickly become a good friend. I flew to Chicago for the Pre-Service Orientation and to learn about VISTA. The training and orientation were incredible; I felt like I found a group of peers, a group of people who were like-minded and wanted to make a difference. Through Pre-Service Orientation I learned about National Service, how it started, the impact it was making and how across the nation individuals were stepping up; "Together We Can Make a Difference." I left the training feeling inspired and I flew back to Omaha excited to learn what the American Red Cross had in store for me.

> I flew to Chicago for the Pre-Service Orientation and to learn about VISTA. The training and orientation were incredible; I felt like I found a group of peers, a group of people who were like-minded and wanted to make a difference.

In my role as an AmeriCorps VISTA I worked with the "Together We Can Make a Difference" program. I started the process of organizing a volunteer database and gave a presentation to the community on how to be better prepared for a disaster. As my year moved along, I gave more presentations to the community, recruited volunteers, and performed general outreach on behalf of the American Red Cross. I admired the passion brought to the organization by the staff and volunteers. The mission of the Red Cross: helping the community prevent, prepare for, and respond to emergencies, became an integral part of my life. As my service year came to a close I considered the next step and turned to Paige for her guidance and direction. She encouraged me to continue on a national service path and also made a move of her own to Denver, Colorado. The year had been difficult financially and personally as my mom had been diagnosed with liver cancer and was struggling through chemo treatments. It was clear I needed to return home to Michigan, but National Service was still on my mind. I started doing some research and came across an opportunity for an AmeriCorps VISTA Leader position with Volunteer Centers of Michigan. I applied and was fortunately offered the position.

> " My roots in service were deep. As I went on through the years working for the American Red Cross, AmeriCorps never drifted far from my thoughts. At every opportunity I promoted service and encouraged others to do so as well. "

In 2004, my term with the Volunteer Centers of Michigan expanded my network of National Service. I gained more knowledge about volunteer recruitment, training, and retention. While I learned valuable skills as a VISTA Leader my heart was still drawn to the American Red Cross and as the term drew near a close I started applying for staff positions. As fate would have it, my chapter back in Iowa needed someone. I interviewed with the Loess Hills chapter and returned to Michigan to await the decision. A few weeks later I received the call and accepted an offer to join their staff. I arrived back at the Iowa chapter just after Hurricane Katrina had hit New Orleans, leaving the area in devastation. Many staff and volunteers had been deployed to help and everyone back in the office was focusing on one aspect or another of the disaster. I stepped right in to a role in health, safety and youth services.

I thought back on how thankful I was for my roles in National Service. I reflected on the people National Service had brought into my life: people like Emily who went on to work for the YMCA, people like Paige who worked with the American Red Cross until she unfortunately and unexpectedly passed away in January of 2014, people like Sheralynn who became a life-long best friend. My roots in service were deep. As I went on through the years working for the American Red Cross, AmeriCorps never drifted far from my thoughts. At every opportunity I promoted service and encouraged others to do so as well.

As the years went by and the economy struggled I moved locations within the Red Cross, working in a chapter in Jackson, MI and then in Chicago, IL. It was in Chicago that the opportunity to run an AmeriCorps program was presented to me. I couldn't contain my excitement at the opportunity to combine what had become my two biggest passions, National Service and American Red Cross. It is so cliché, but I felt like this job had been created just for me, so in 2009 I took over the Chicago Safe Families AmeriCorps program. I worked with a team of 18 members across Illinois, based mainly in Chicago. It was a learning experience being on the other side of the AmeriCorps experience. My training had prepared me well for the program I was about to take on, but I also had no idea what running an AmeriCorps program truly entailed.

With the birth of my daughter in 2011, Michigan was calling me home because I wanted her to be around family and friends. Once again luck was on my side; the AmeriCorps Program Director in Michigan had just given notice he would be leaving his position for a new opportunity. In what seemed like a whirlwind, I applied, interviewed, was offered and accepted the position as the new AmeriCorps Program Director for the "Together We Prepare" AmeriCorps program in Michigan. I began working with a new team in the fall of 2011. Today, I love my work and I love to see the difference my team makes. I just completed training with a third team since I have been with the Michigan program. The teams have gone on to train thousands of people on how to be better prepared for a disaster and have recruited over 1,000 new volunteers in Michigan to serve the American Red Cross mission. In 2014 we hope to reach over 30,000 individuals and recruit 1,500 volunteers.

Ten years ago I had never heard of AmeriCorps, not knowing that I could do something in life I loved and that made a difference in the lives of those around me. When I was in school no one mentioned a career with the American Red Cross, in fact no one ever mentioned the non-profit world at all. While we've come a long way in those ten years, it still saddens me to see blank faces when I mention AmeriCorps. It saddens me that we'll be enrolling our millionth member in 2014 and still so many people ask me what the "A" stands for on my shirt. While the public might not know what our members are doing, we continue to educate the nation. It feels good to know there are members all over this nation serving in their communities and working together to "Get Things Done!"

BETSY LAAKSO is continuing a life dedicated to National Service as the National Services Director for the American Red Cross. If you'd like to know more you can contact Betsy at betsy.laakso@gmail.com. This chapter has been dedicated to the memory of Paige Thomas, a friend who stood apart from others in the world with her uninhibited spirit and relaxed nature.

A Passion Ignited

By Melissa Grober-Morrow

Served as a VISTA at the Urban Education
Institute at the University of Chicago
Chicago, Illinois

I didn't come from a family that volunteered. I started volunteering in high school because it was a requirement of the honors society. When I got to college, it just seemed natural to continue. I explored different options by volunteering in a mental health institution, a health clinic, and a tutoring program. All of these experiences helped me grow, but they also showed me what I didn't want to do; none of them were the right fit. All I knew was I wanted to work in a field that helped people. I had been interested in working for a nonprofit organization—I thought maybe that was the right direction—but had little experience with nonprofits and wasn't sure how to go about getting a job in the sector. I also wanted to experience life in another city. I no longer remember how I first heard about AmeriCorps, but the more I looked into it, the more it seemed like a worthwhile endeavor. At the end of college, I applied for AmeriCorps positions in Chicago and New Orleans—cities I had never visited— ultimately deciding to go to Chicago. I didn't know anything about the differences between AmeriCorps programs, so I applied to AmeriCorps national and VISTA programs. All the while, my family wondered why I—or anyone, for that matter—would serve full-time.

I decided to take an AmeriCorps VISTA position with the University of Chicago's Urban Education Institute (then the Center for School Improvement). Through that program, my fellow AmeriCorps members and I were placed in public elementary schools throughout Chicago's low-income neighborhoods to run the STEP reading program for kids in kindergarten through third grade. We worked with AmeriCorps state members, who served as the reading partners and tutors in the program. With my conversational Spanish skills, I was placed at a school in a large Latino community.

> All the while, my family wondered why I—or anyone, for that matter—would serve full-time.

The principal of my school tasked me with the parents, and running the STEP reading program. I knew nothing about parent engagement, but I saw caring, loving parents dropping off their children every day. I went to work assessing the school environment and resources offered for parents. The school lacked a parent-teacher organization, so I set up a parent advisory council. Many of the parents had limited English skills. They were grateful for my attempts to speak to them in Spanish and to draw them into the school. We had a few parents who volunteered regularly. I befriended them and enlisted their help to determine what would bring more parents to meetings. I printed flyers advertising meetings in English and Spanish and my mom helped translate materials for the Spanish-speaking parent population. I positioned the parents as leaders of the meetings, giving them ownership of the council.

I partnered with local community development corporations, which agreed to offer English classes at the school for parents during the school day. Knowing that many students' parents lacked a high school diploma, I sought to bring in GED classes and partnered with an organization that provided refurbished computers at low cost to families. I also brought workshops to the school teaching adults how to read with their children. My fellow AmeriCorps members and I hosted a health fair at school to position it as the center of the community. I came to view the parents of the school as friends. They so clearly wanted what was best for their children, but they often lacked the financial and educational resources needed to counteract negative influences of the surrounding community.

Moreover, they were appreciative of any help my fellow AmeriCorps members and I offered.

The principal at my school gave me flexibility to do what I thought would best serve the community. I was grateful for her trust and partnership at school. I had a great year supporting students and parents at Cameron Elementary School. I loved drawing parents into the school, providing them with resources and helping them connect with their kids. Focus on parents also helped improve reading levels for students as an added benefit.

It turned out AmeriCorps VISTA had been the perfect way to launch my career in the nonprofit sector. I learned from this experience that I really enjoy developing programs and providing services to build capacity within communities and I've been trying to continue this work ever since.

My VISTA experience made me believe in the power of schools beyond their ability to teach our children. Schools can serve as an important and safe space not just for students, but also for the neighborhood and community that supports them. VISTA allowed me to learn about the challenges many schools have when trying to engage parents in their children's education. My experience also allowed me to gain a deeper understanding of poverty, as well as policies and practices that affect children and parents. My service was fundamentally transformational for me and I hope it has made a long-lasting impression in the communities I have served.

The valuable experience I had as an AmeriCorps VISTA member brought me on a winding path to my current job running national programs that support financial capability for low-income people around the country. Without my VISTA experience, I would not have learned that I enjoy developing evidence-based programs responsive to community needs that also engage the community to drive solutions.

> " My VISTA experience made me believe in the power of schools beyond their ability to teach our children. Schools can serve as an important and safe space not just for students, but also for the neighborhood and community that supports them. "

I also learned a lot about myself while serving as a VISTA. Had I not served, it might have taken years of trials and error to discover what jobs I did not want. My VISTA experience showed me that I thrive most in entrepreneurial environments strengthening communities and building programs, I understand clearly how community volunteers have the opportunity to be problem solvers.

My family still doesn't quite "get" volunteering and nonprofit work. For most of them, work is a paycheck and a means to an end. For me, a career in service can—and must be—so much more. I am fortunate to have had this deep learning experience so early in my career.

MELISSA GROBER-MORROW is Senior Director of Economic Opportunity Programs at Points of Light, where she runs national AmeriCorps VISTA programs. When she's not working, she can be found teaching yoga or singing. She currently lives in Birmingham, AL with her husband, son, and dog.

Because Anybody Can Serve

By Jessi Pryor

Served in NCCC at the Southeast Campus
Charleston, South Carolina

hen I started my 10 months of service it was September 25th, 2001 and only 14 days since our country was rocked by the terrorist attack in New York City on 9/11. I had signed up for AmeriCorps National Civilian Community Corps (NCCC) earlier that summer when life was a little simpler and less scary. With my brand new shiny undergraduate degree in sociology behind me, I kept questioning what was next for me. After all, what do you do with a sociology degree? In the meantime, I was enjoying my 4th summer working at a local theme park in Branson, Missouri. Life was good. Then 9/11 happened. I could have backed out and started graduate school, but I knew I needed this chance, this opportunity to figure out who I was. I wouldn't have even known what kind of graduate degree I wanted to pursue at that point. Like many I met in AmeriCorps, I needed to figure out what I wanted to do with my life and I felt deep down this time away from home and out of my comfort zone would guide me. I found myself leaving my little bubble and the safety of the Ozark Mountains and heading East with absolutely no clue what was ahead.

I remember pulling into the old Naval base in Charleston, South Carolina and thinking, "What a strange place." Because of 9/11, the security was tight and there were armed guards at the gate. The base still housed the Coast Guard, the Border Patrol Academy and AmeriCorps

NCCC. It had been formally closed in the 90s and had colossal buildings sitting empty and rows and rows of officer housing that resembled a ghost town. I remember thinking, "Where am I?" I knew everything would be okay because after all, I had volunteered before right? I had planted a few trees at my high school and picked up trash on the adopt-a-highway stretch for my church. Early on, my dad had taught me the importance of service and I often tagged along when he did a landscaping project for our church or assisted an elderly person in the community. Ten months of helping others, ten months of traveling and seeing the southeast United States, ten months that changed my life. "I can do this," I thought.

Within a few weeks, our team, Blue Seven, had completed the team building exercises and began our first project. We remained local and assisted teachers as in-class aides and after school tutors for an elementary school in North Charleston. My parents were both educators, so this assignment felt natural. I remember the joy I felt when the kids were excited to see us and for us to simply pay attention to them. I worked in a 2nd grade classroom with a young teacher who had her hands full. The school was considered at-risk and low income and our team provided the extra eyes, ears and words of encouragement these kids needed. Working in this diverse community as a minority taught me a great deal about acceptance, tolerance and ignoring differences. This would prove invaluable as I later chose my career as a social worker. I left this project very optimistic and wondering if I, too, had a place someday working at a school.

In addition to the larger projects, we were also expected to perform smaller service projects and volunteer hours in the communities where we were assigned. One that stands out to me is the day our team of twelve, nine women and three men, loaded up in the fifteen passenger van and drove to a rural area outside of Charleston to paint an elderly couple's home. We learned quickly this wasn't an ordinary house or an ordinary project. Our team was still getting to know each other and figuring out what skills were brought to the table. When you put twelve people from all over the United States, ages varying from 18-24 and in different stages of their lives and educations, things are going to be interesting.

As the muggy Carolina heat bore down on us, we scraped the gray cinder block house, prepped it for paint and evolved as a team. The elderly couple provided abundant sweet tea to quench our thirst. Even though we simply painted the old cinder block house, you would have thought we built them a brand new house. They wanted to thank us at the end of the day by preparing a meal. They didn't have much money and wanted to show their appreciation for our days work. As we sat at the dining room table with paint in our hair and on our face, we shared a meal as a team and with this couple. That memory has stuck with me for over 12 years.

Back on base, other teams were being sent to New York City to assist the Red Cross and other agencies responding to 9/11. I wanted so badly for our team to be picked, but the thought of going scared me to death. One girl on our team was from New Jersey and she and I later took a road trip during our Easter break to NYC to see her parents and to show me the city. As we stood in front of the massive hole where the Twin Towers once stood and gazed at the two single blue lights illuminating the sky, she reflected how surreal it was for them to no longer be there. She had been to the top of them and now, just like that, they were gone. To stand with her in front of this hallowed ground, I knew I was exactly where I belonged and although sad, the experience energized me for the remainder of our service. Even if my team wasn't assigned to that project, I was proud we had fellow Corps members providing assistance.

> " As we sat at the dining room table with paint in our hair and on our face, we shared a meal as a team and with this couple. That memory has stuck with me for over 12 years. "

Throughout the 10 months of service, we left Charleston for projects in Georgia, Alabama, Florida and West Virginia. We worked for state park organizations, Habitat for Humanity, the Nature Conservancy, YMCA and the Red Cross. I was getting serious on-the-job training in construction, exotic plant removal, trail building and disaster relief. In each town and on each project, our team met people and communities that without our help, would have had to rely on private funding or tap into tight budgets to get the work we were completing done.

We made a day trip over to Atlanta to visit the grave of Dr. Martin

Luther King Jr. while we were working on an environmental project in Georgia. Talking about service, Dr. King once said, "Everybody can be great, because anybody can serve. You don't have to have a college degree to serve. You don't have to make your subject and verb agree to serve. You only need a heart full of grace. A soul generated by love." This resonated with me and I took those words to heart. It was around this time I knew when I returned to Missouri that I wanted to pursue a graduate degree in Social Work. But the year wasn't over yet and there was plenty left to do before I made that leap.

> My training and experience in AmeriCorps NCCC made me better prepared to assist those in crisis and I did my best to try to bring them some comfort.

We encountered extreme poverty in the hills of West Virginia when we were assigned to assist the Red Cross on a disaster relief project. There had been a terrible flash flood and many residents were displaced from their homes, some having been completely washed away. Our task was to work in the relief centers and conduct intake interviews for persons affected. We also went out into the communities and met with those who had no way to get to us. Because of my experience on this project, I chose to do an internship as a disaster relief caseworker with my local Red Cross during my graduate studies. During this time, I recognized the panic and desperation in the eyes of those asking for help, just like the residents of rural West Virginia. My training and experience in AmeriCorps NCCC made me better prepared to assist those in crisis and I did my best to try to bring them some comfort.

After our time in West Virginia our team ended our service by working for a YMCA Nature Camp just north of Charleston. For the next two months, we acted as camp counselors for inner city youth, who spent a week in our care. This project was especially fun since it was just like playing for two months! Being a gal from the Ozarks, I was assigned to the fishing pond and taught kids how to fish and identify the other critters found in the camp pond. Our time at the camp ended and as we wrapped up our 10 months and prepared for graduation in July, I looked back in awe at all we had accomplished in such a short period of time. I made life long friends and to this day, I stay in touch with many of my teammates from Blue Seven.

Two years later, with my Masters in Social Work behind me, I took a job as a school social worker for the local public school district in Springfield, MO. The three K-5 elementary schools I served were considered to be at-risk and in lower-income neighborhoods, just like our school in North Charleston. It was during this time I realized my time of service with AmeriCorps had given me the courage and confidence to dig deep and really try to reach these children that needed help with social skills, depression and behavior problems. I had used my education award wisely. I developed my skills as a counselor and provided character education and team building lessons during the after school programs, in addition to partnering with the school counselor and leading small groups throughout the school day. I continued in this role for nearly four years until the grant funded position came to a close. Although I was leaving, I tried my hand at grant writing to bring AmeriCorps VISTA workers into the schools. I laid the groundwork for the administrators to follow up and keep service alive.

During this time also, newly formed AmeriCorps Alums called for volunteers in the wake of Hurricane Katrina and requested alums to come to New Orleans to help. It was May 2006, and the flood waters were long gone but the city remained in devastation. I felt called to go and raised enough gas money from fellow school employees to get myself and a former NCCC team member, Kayla Humiston, there. We were assigned to partner with Hands On Network of New Orleans and Gulf Coast and spent a week of gutting homes and clean up. It was exhausting and frankly disgusting work. While there, we met current NCCC members and other alums and swapped stories of service. There is a bond that we all share and when you've been in the trenches together, you just get it. I was impacted in a way I simply cannot put into words when I saw the areas in New Orleans where homes once stood. A week was all I could give at this particular stage in my life, but it felt good to be part of the relief effort.

Hearing I was nearly out of a job, a friend who worked as a dialysis social worker called to say there was a position in the company she worked for and I should apply. I applied and began a six year period working with those on kidney dialysis. I organized teams for the National Kidney Foundation's annual Kidney Walk, worked in the community to raise awareness about End Stage Renal Disease, and educated patients how to secure financial assistance for medications, transportation and kidney transplant expenses. I worked to empower the patients to take better care of themselves and assisted patients and their loved ones in finding primary care physicians so they could treat their diabetes and high blood pressure and hopefully prevent further progression of the disease. It was during this time I obtained my Licensed Clinical Social Worker certification and utilized my skills to address the underlying issues and barriers to why patients missed their life sustaining treatments and to address their quality of life concerns.

> AmeriCorps significantly changed my life. It helped me to become confident that I could make a difference, no matter how small. I plan to keep service a part of my life forever and to teach my children to do the same.

Perhaps the most unique benefit I received from my time with NCCC is that I met my husband while serving. He was not in AmeriCorps at the time, but training on the base in Charleston for a separate agency. We recently celebrated five years of marriage and the birth of our first child and in recent years have returned to Charleston, our favorite city, for our honeymoon and babymoon. Currently, I am blessed to be a stay-at-home mom, which allows me to continue exploring volunteer opportunities with my local AmeriCorps Alums chapter and the national chapter to speak at career fairs and recruit the next generation of AmeriCorps leaders. AmeriCorps significantly changed my life. It helped me to become confident that I could make a difference, no matter how small. I plan to keep service a part of my life forever and to teach my children to do the same.

JESSI PRYOR is currently a stay at home mom pursuing a leadership role with her local AmeriCorps Alums Chapter. Prior to the birth of her son, she worked as a dialysis social worker and school social worker.

Serving So Others Can Serve

. . . .

By **Marley Balasco**

Served as a VISTA with Vermont Youth Development
Corps at the University of Vermont 4H extension
Vermont Operation: Military Kids
Burlington, Vermont

S ervice has always been a passion of mine. From a young age I knew I wanted to serve others with my career. Throughout my life I found that the people I came in contact with, who worked in the non-profit field, tended to be selfless, energetic and happy people. I aspired to be like this as well. Individuals who worked in nonprofits tended to have a dedication to their work and a commitment to enact change. As I grew older I wanted to surround myself with individuals that sought to edify others because I wished to do the same in my life. I wanted to be a part of something where this was the goal.

AmeriCorps provided this opportunity. On a personal level I could explore the career field I was interested in while also gaining practical experience. Even more exciting, I could belong to something that sought to edify others and build into communities. I have served in several youth development programs including at camps, school tutoring programs and coaching various sports teams. I knew youth development was the correct path for me so I applied to youth programs throughout the country focusing on those geared towards community engagement. This aspect of any AmeriCorps job was nonnegotiable for me. I am, and always have been, a firm believer that the most natural learning occurs when youth are given something to do, rather than simply learn. I wanted a hands-on program.

> "As I grew older I wanted to surround myself with individuals that sought to edify others because I wished to do the same in my life. I wanted to be a part of something where this was the goal."

Originally I am from Barrington, Rhode Island, but attended college at Norwich University, a military college based in Northfield, Vermont. The student body is made up of a large population of Reserve Officer's Training Corps (ROTC) students. ROTC is a college-based program that trains prospective officers of the United States Armed Forces. Even though I applied to programs all over the country I was drawn to a local Vermont program close to my college town.

I accepted a position with Vermont Youth Development Corps and was placed at the University of Vermont 4-H Operation: Military Kids in Burlington, Vermont. I had a persistent offer from another social services program, but believed the position with Operation Military Kids would be the most natural fit. It helped that this program was only 45 minutes away from my alma mater and that I had fantastic relationships with university faculty, staff, and other students. Given that Operation Military Kids aims to serve youth of military families, I thought my connection to Norwich University and their ROTC population would provide excellent opportunities for the students, school, and program participants alike by establishing a relationship.

The decision to accept the position with Operation Military Kids turned out to be one of the best choices of my life. The highlight of my service time came when Norwich University and I were able to provide military youth the opportunity to enjoy a Military Youth day on campus. I had the privilege of creating a team of eight student-athletes who gave their time to fundraise, organize, promote and recruit volunteers for the Military Youth Day. Youth participants from around the state of Vermont attended the event. They spent the day playing games, eating ice cream and enjoying campus with fifteen student-athlete volunteers, eight of whom were ROTC students themselves. Having the participants and volunteers share military backgrounds provided a safe space for everyone allowing student volunteers to comfort children of the National Guardsmen Stationed overseas.

This experience and many others helped shape my life in overwhelmingly positive ways. Before serving with AmeriCorps, I always thought that, in service, the overall goal should be to "save the world," to think on the largest scale possible. Very early in my service I realized this view needed to change. In the military there is this thing called the "deployment cycle." In Vermont, the effects of deployment may be more apparent to the outside world because all service members are part of the National Guard. Whereas most states have a base that is assigned to the Navy or Air Force and so on, these service members don't have access to a base. Apart from weekend drills every two months, National Guard members are essentially living "normal, civilian lifestyle" until their unit is given a deployment date. This is when the cycle begins. There are many difficulties and concerns that come with deployment. Not just for the service members but also for the family and loved ones they leave behind.

When a loved one is deployed, other family members must step up and take on new roles and try to create a new sense of normalcy. For example, it might be normal for a mom to prepare dinner for her family. However, if she gets deployed someone new needs to take on that role. It might be the father or children will begin to prepare their own meals.

The topic of deployment cycle was addressed at an event for Yellow Ribbon, an organization that promotes the well being of National Guard and Reserve members, their families and communities, by connecting them with different resources throughout deployment cycles. Local resources are available to service members and their loved ones before, during, and after deployments.

On the morning of the Yellow Ribbon event, I provided science experiments for children with family in the military. We had an amazing morning of popping caps off film canisters using different amounts of alka seltzer tablets. The youth always enjoyed this activity but there was more to it than just fun. After the activities were complete, we finished the program with thoughtful question and answer times designed to help children reflect on various aspects of having a family member in the military.

During this particular event I posed this question to the group: "Today you had the opportunity to take on the role of a scientist. During your family member's deployment, can you recall a time when you had to take on a new role like you did today?" This response from a five year old stands out, "When I would go to bed, my daddy would turn off my light. Then I had to do it myself." It was such a simple thing. It was not a change her mom seemed to notice, but it had a huge impact in the life of this little girl. This experience struck me so significantly because it served as a reminder that the smallest details can have a great impact on an individual; especially in the life of a child. Collectively as communities we have opportunities, no matter how small, to come around military families and support them when loved ones are deployed. As this little girl so sweetly expressed, it can be small things that help provide normalcy in a tumultuous time.

Since my service with AmeriCorps ended, I have continued to pursue my passions for youth development. Currently, I work with children who have been diagnosed with Autism. Part of my work includes helping students develop life skills as well as providing resources and different ways to get students more involved in their communities. Long-term, I hope to establish community based youth programming that promotes life skills including civic engagement. No matter where I end up, I will always aim to provide awareness of challenges facing military families in the communities where I live. My time with AmeriCorps and Operation Military Kids had a profound impact on my life. It solidified my passion for youth work and it made me aware that even the smallest actions can create a large change.

> "Collectively as communities we have opportunities, no matter how small, to come around military families and support them when loved ones are deployed."

MARLEY BALASCO hopes to eventually start a non-profit that works to promote community based youth programming promoting life skills in underserved youth.

Community is the Center of Service

By **Eric Shovein**

Served in an AmeriCorps State Program
with the Power of We Consortium
at the Ingham County Land Bank
Lansing, Michigan

I started a yearlong AmeriCorps term in 2009 and it changed my life by allowing me to invest in the lives of others. I served at the Ingham County Land Bank in order to create its Garden Program. The program itself is called the "Power of We Consortium" and is based out of Lansing, Michigan. This is one of the more synergistic areas to work in the food system given its proximity to Michigan State University, a school known for its agricultural program.

Instead of just looking at the experience at my site, I think it's important to talk about what led me to serve as an AmeriCorps member and where serving in AmeriCorps has taken me since my service ended. This is important because I believe AmeriCorps is very under-emphasized as an option to open up future opportunities, when it is in reality one of the best first steps to take if you plan to have a career dedicated to public service. Not enough people know this program.

The End of College, Peace Corps, and the Search for Domestic Alternatives

To be frank, AmeriCorps was never on my radar in college. I remember going to the career fair at the University of Michigan as a junior and gravitating directly to the Peace Corps table. I ultimately ended up joining the Peace Corps and moved to Cambodia to teach English after my senior year. To this day, I am sure that the decision to join Peace Corps was at least a little bit path-dependent because of the marketing surrounding Peace Corps and lack thereof surrounding AmeriCorps. Building on that idea, Peace Corps seemed exotic, in that it opened travel to a foreign land while learning about a new culture. It was an opportunity to make a difference. AmeriCorps, on the other hand, was shrouded in mystery. As soon as I got back to the United States after a short time in Peace Corps Cambodia, I knew I wanted to stay in public service so I started to look for domestic alternatives.

My AmeriCorps Experience

My AmeriCorps program took me to Lansing, a rustbelt city in Michigan with large economic issues partially driven by the decline of the domestic auto industry. For that reason, there were many needs in the city, given a large amount of joblessness and poverty. My program directly addressed the issues regarding food security and access to green space. We had people serving in numerous food banks throughout the region. One worked in a gardening program servicing a food bank while another worked on a small farm with juveniles who had discipline issues, and my position with the Ingham County Land Bank.

The very first day at the site, I was nervous about a yearlong project and my fears were anything but assuaged. I knew nothing about gardens, nothing about community work, and nothing about Lansing. Sure I had planted a seed or two in my lifetime, probably in elementary school as a project, and I helped transplant flowers for my mother on mother's day in the past. That was, however, the extent of my knowledge and here I was in charge of a program.

In spite of such inexperience, my supervisor did not seem to worry. A very laidback guy, he said he hired me because I "seemed like a self-starter." I asked him if there was any direction or papers to guide me. There were not. I did however find a "stack" of about 5 pages of paper from past interns sitting on a table next to my computer.

This is not completely typical for an AmeriCorps program, but each site varies. As I look back, I could not have been happier with my placement. Even with no gardening experience, my site supervisor allowed me to create a business plan. After doing the necessary research, I was allowed to implement and operate the program however I saw fit. I started by creating a calendar for the next year. The first few months were entirely dedicated to research and planning while spring would be dedicated to acquiring materials for the gardens and summer would be dedicated to gardening.

Throughout the winter I spent months learning each detail of gardening such as, when cool weather crops should be planted and when summer crops should be planted. I researched grant programs for free seeds, which nonprofits in the area gave out plant starts and how to expand each program. I solicited donations for compost, researched tilling and got in touch with master gardeners in order to find a rain barrel workshop allowing gardeners to have a free water source.

However, the most fulfilling and challenging part was integrating into the community to find participants for gardens. To do this, I first had to master the geographic location of each vacant parcel in Lansing. I then had to survey each parcel in order to see what parcels had adequate southern sun and were suitable to become gardens. From there, I had to find lists of each neighborhood group, every block club, community center, and each owner of a home next to a vacant parcel.

The neighborhood group research dominated the largest part of my time because without participants, nothing else mattered. I contacted the leader of each neighborhood association and scheduled a date to talk about the garden program I was starting. Sometimes one person would show up, sometimes a handful.

Networking in the community quickly became my favorite part of service. Most people didn't trust a program giving out free materials so I had to build trust. In order to build trust, I had to keep an open ear, to listen to the stories of struggle. One gardener was a Vietnam veteran burned while in service to his country. He suffered pain "at a level of 7 out of 10" on a daily basis. Gardening however put him at peace and he just wanted to share his story with someone who would listen. As the year went on, I saw him on a regular basis, often in his garden, showing off his harvest.

> People wanted to share their lives, and the more they did, the harder they worked. The relationships were as important as the gardens.

I had another gardener who created a micro-community center. He dedicated his entire life to helping his multi-ethnic block, making sure children had books to read, toys to play with, technology to learn from, and a safe place to do it all. He rehabbed an entire house to provide that safe place. He also saw gardening as a crucial piece of this puzzle and years later he continues a garden on his block.

The interaction with gardeners turned out to be the highlight of my service. People wanted to share their lives, and the more they did, the harder they worked. The relationships were as important as the gardens. The more I asked questions and cared, the more they wanted to garden. They believed in the benefits of growing food for themselves and their community. By the time spring came around, there were 20 family or community gardens that fed hundreds of people.

During the summer, I had another AmeriCorps member working with me who was a liaison for some of the gardens. This allowed me to spend my time at The Urbandale Farm Project. With the help of two MSU professors and other AmeriCorps members, I helped start this farm as a part of the program. This project encouraged community involvement and we would open the farm whenever we were working. With so many volunteers we were able to sell produce at a discounted rate. The entire program ended up being an overwhelming success and has expanded in the years since. It was able to put plenty of healthy vegetables into the homes of underserved community members and beautified neighborhoods by using lots. Having such success, such richness of relationships, I knew I wanted to give my life to public service after my AmeriCorps term.

My Experiences After & Thanks to AmeriCorps

The first step after my life in AmeriCorps was a move to the Caribbean to teach English through the French government. After a year I returned to Detroit to do a summer AmeriCorps term at Development Centers Inc. on Detroit's Westside. I then went on to law school. Like my past service in Lansing, gardening was again part of the focus in the Detroit program, with an emphasis on Early Childhood Education.

My site was primarily situated near one of Detroit's most impoverished neighborhoods: Brightmoor. With their parents by their side, we would put on playgroups and activities for children up to the age of five.

When the term finished, I used my AmeriCorps experience as a catalyst to law school. I wanted to continue work that benefited underserved, diverse communities. Accordingly I chose anti-torture, refugee, and asylum work. I found my AmeriCorps experience not only made me a more effective advocate for distressed clients, the community from AmeriCorps actually opened doors.

Seeking refugee status in the United States (asylum applicants are included within this category) means someone has been persecuted on the basis of race, religion, nationality, political opinion, or for being a part of a particular social group. It should come as no surprise clients of this type of law are underprivileged. Many clients have literally fled their homes and fear for their lives. All they have is a suitcase of clothes and a handful of documents (if they are lucky) when they arrive in the United States. Also, it is not surprising that the listening skills I honed in AmeriCorps proved to be invaluable when working with this population. Being able to actively listen and build trust with people from all backgrounds made my job has significantly easier. Because client's fears are diminished, the adjudicator's job of capturing their stories becomes easier.

One of my favorite parts of the public service work is truly believing people I serve are my heroes. They are the people when trapped in a bad situation do not give up, but find a way to succeed against societal odds. This is especially true with refugee and asylum work where clients have literally stood up for their opinion or rights even in the face of death.

AmeriCorps service has also opened up other professional doors. For example, in addition to the refugee and asylum work, I had an opportunity to do anti-torture work in Kolkata, India. After my first year of law school, I applied for a fellowship and moved to India to work in anti-torture law.

> AmeriCorps helped open my eyes to other cultures and people as well as provided an opportunity for me to gain leadership skills.

Far from just moving into an area as an outsider for the summer, I actually integrated into the local community. I joined the local soccer team and made friends, most of whom did not speak more than five words of English. By the end of the three months working in India, there were a handful of people who felt like family.

Another advantage of AmeriCorps expressed itself when interviewing victims of torture on the India-Bangladesh border. At that point, I had not done any other internship in law school, so I relied solely on past experiences including the times I spoke to community groups about gardens in Michigan. AmeriCorps helped open my eyes to other cultures and people as well as provided an opportunity for me to gain leadership skills. I will continue to use everything I learned in the future and I hope to grow the leadership qualities planted in me from my first AmeriCorps position.

ERIC SHOVEIN recently finished his J.D. at Wayne State University Law School and moved onto the finalist stage of the Presidential Management Fellowship. He is currently trying to find an agency placement in the federal government allowing continued service.

Endnotes

1   Steven Waldman, *The Bill*, New York, Penguin, 1995, p. 20
2   Portions of the following are adapted from David Reingold and Leslie Lenkowsky, "The Future of National Service," *Public Administration Review*, Issue Supplement S1, December 2010, pp. s114- s121.
3   Shirley Sagawa, *The American Way to Change: How National Service and Volunteers are Transforming America*, San Francisco, Jossey-Bass, 2010.

KATE CAMARA is an English Literature graduate of Taylor University. She currently lives in New York City where she is an intern at Hephzibah House. Through this ministry she offers free English as Second Language (ESL) classes to the community. She also works part time as an ESL teacher in Time Square. Through Indiana University's distance education program Kate is working on her Masters in Language Education.

ERIC NELSON WALTON is currently living in Indianapolis as an artist, illustrator, designer, and photographer. He hopes all of his work shows that truth is harsh, raw, and beautiful.

Thank you to everyone who helped make this book a reality. I would like to extend extra appreciation towards my mother Becky, my father Keith and my Aunt Beth. Your insight and support have been invaluable. Thank you also to Nicole Adams for graciously taking letter pictures. Your friendship means the world.

Rachel

CPSIA information can be obtained
at www.ICGtesting.com
Printed in the USA
FFOW03n2004081014
7913FF